# Praise for *Conscious Writing*:

'Writing Notes from the Universe, *I know what it feels like when the words come through me, rather than from me; when they are my own, yet deeper; when the art of writing starts surprising you. Julia's Conscious Writing reveals how to reach the inner state that is outside space and time to write that way consistently. If you have a message to share, read this book!'*
MIKE DOOLEY, *NEW YORK TIMES* BESTSELLING AUTHOR AND ENTREPRENEUR

'This extraordinary book about conscious writing deserves a place on the shelf next to Writing Down the Bones, Bird by Bird and The Artist's Way. Practical, profound and insightfully written, McCutchen's guide to creative awakening through spiritual awareness is a must-read for anyone interested in finding their voice and learning how to use it...McCutchen, a former publishing executive, earned her wisdom the old-fashioned way, through decades of creative trial and error - including life-changing personal loss - which is why Conscious Writing has the ring of truth. I will read it again and again.'
MARK MATOUSEK, AUTHOR OF *ETHICAL WISDOM, WHEN YOU'RE FALLING, DIVE* AND *WRITING TO AWAKEN*

'Writing is only incidentally about words – it is more fundamentally about showing up, paying attention, being authentic – and growing conscious. All this Julia McCutchen explains beautifully in her new book, Conscious Writing. Don't miss it!'
ERIC MAISEL, CREATIVITY COACH AND AUTHOR OF *COACHING THE ARTIST WITHIN*

'Julia's own expansion of consciousness is here beautifully and brilliantly shared through her creative passion of writing. This refreshingly holistic approach will serve writers of all kinds in their quest to write from their heart with a true voice. ...Her clear, inspiring and practical guidance offers great and timely value for...creatively authentic expressions of the heart, mind and soul. Ultimately, this teaching applies to the wholeness of experiencing and embodying a fully conscious life.'
DR JUDE CURRIVAN, COSMOLOGIST, HEALER AND AUTHOR OF *HOPE: HEALING OUR PEOPLE & EARTH*

'A beautiful and profound exploration of the close connection between spirituality and creativity, full of practical exercises which will help to release your own creative potential and enrich your life as a whole.'
STEVE TAYLOR PhD, AUTHOR OF *WAKING FROM SLEEP* AND *THE CALM CENTER*

'Human creativity has two components: logos and mythos. We scientists explain the creative process, the flow experience and all that, but that's all logos. What the creative does with his/her creativity – the creative journey – is the unveiling of the all-important mythos. How to travel your mythical journey consciously is the subject of Julia McCutchen's exciting book. Read and enjoy: this book will put you in readiness for your creative journey. I guarantee it.'
AMIT GOSWAMI PhD, AUTHOR OF *QUANTUM CREATIVITY* AND *QUANTUM ECONOMICS*

# CONSCIOUS
# WRITING

By the same author:

*The Writer's Journey: From Inspiration to Publication*

# CONSCIOUS
# WRITING

## Discover Your True Voice
## Through Mindfulness and More

Julia McCutchen

**HAY HOUSE**

Carlsbad, California • New York City • London • Sydney
Johannesburg • Vancouver • Hong Kong • New Delhi

First published and distributed in the United Kingdom by:
Hay House UK Ltd, Astley House, 33 Notting Hill Gate, London W11 3JQ
Tel: +44 (0)20 3675 2450; Fax: +44 (0)20 3675 2451; www.hayhouse.co.uk

Published and distributed in the United States of America by:
Hay House Inc., PO Box 5100, Carlsbad, CA 92018-5100
Tel: (1) 760 431 7695 or (800) 654 5126; Fax: (1) 760 431 6948 or (800) 650 5115
www.hayhouse.com

Published and distributed in Australia by:
Hay House Australia Ltd, 18/36 Ralph St, Alexandria NSW 2015
Tel: (61) 2 9669 4299; Fax: (61) 2 9669 4144; www.hayhouse.com.au

Published and distributed in the Republic of South Africa by:
Hay House SA (Pty) Ltd, PO Box 990, Witkoppen 2068
info@hayhouse.co.za; www.hayhouse.co.za

Published and distributed in India by:
Hay House Publishers India, Muskaan Complex, Plot No.3, B-2,
Vasant Kunj, New Delhi 110 070
Tel: (91) 11 4176 1620; Fax: (91) 11 4176 1630; www.hayhouse.co.in

Distributed in Canada by:
Raincoast Books, 2440 Viking Way, Richmond, B.C. V6V 1N2
Tel: (1) 604 448 7100; Fax: (1) 604 270 7161; www.raincoast.com

A catalogue record for this book is available from the British Library.

ISBN: 978-1-78180-542-8

Interior images: 1, 67, 109, 157 © KreativKolors/Shutterstock;
34 Thinkstock/stalkerstudent; p.118–119, 133–136 © robloxston.co.uk

Printed and bound in Great Britain by CPI Group (UK) Ltd, Croydon, CR0 4YY

May we all

discover our true voice

and express ourselves

consciously and creatively

in the world.

# Contents

**Part IV: Creating Your Conscious Writing Practice**

# Preface

It's a crystal-clear day with luminous blue skies. The warmth from the sun feels nurturing as I gaze softly into the reflection on the surface of the water. The light shimmers as a breeze whispers through the trees and sends ripples to the distant shore of the wildlife pond.

I'm sitting in my favourite place with a pen and notepad on my lap, playing with words, trying them on like clothes to feel which ones resonate at the deepest level.

Finding the right form to describe the essence of my work in everyday language feels like a stretch. Which words will shine the clearest light into the vastness towards which they point?

I know the essence intuitively. I dance with the energy of it on a daily basis as I journey through the linear time of the everyday world where it takes on the multitude of forms that are the threads that weave my conscious and creative tapestry. While the essence remains unchanged, the forms continue to evolve and become ever more accurate echoes of what lies beyond. Now it is time for the next layer to be revealed.

Poised on the cusp of focus and flow, with clear intent arising from surrender to greater awareness, I remain open. I listen attentively and look beyond the surface for flickers of insight welling up from the depths. I'm immersed in this timeless moment, oblivious to everything else for as long as it takes.

Then clarity arrives in an instant, seemingly from nowhere. The words 'Conscious Writing' flood into my awareness. Immediately I Know. This is it – for now.

This whole-body sense of Knowing includes a feeling of complete alignment which is vibrant and alive. It's a sensation I recognize as an expression of the compelling inner impulse I've been intuitively following for as long as I can remember, and with full awareness since a life-changing accident in 1999.

As managing director and publisher of a medium-sized independent publishing house which specialized in spiritual, personal development and lifestyle books for an international audience, I attended a major sales conference in Cyprus to present the new season's titles. In the opening session, a large stage spotlight accidentally fell and struck me on the crown of the head. It literally took me apart at every level, and that single moment in time changed the course of my life.

My healing journey lasted seven years, during which I became familiar with the darkness of doubt and despair as well as the awe-inspiring influx of light and clarity such an opportunity for awakening provides. The experience triggered a series of quantum leaps in my inner transformation that gradually became reflected in my outer world as I reassembled the pieces of myself and my life from the inside out.

A whole new level of awareness became my default setting and I came to trust implicitly the inner promptings that arose from a deeper level of Knowing beyond my everyday mind, even when I had no idea where they would lead. They remain a guiding force in my life. Consciously working with the alchemy of awakening, intellectual understanding dissolves into living the Truth in each and every moment.

This is the 'conscious' in Conscious Writing. It's about becoming, and remaining, conscious. From this awakening, there arises a natural impulse to create: true self-expression flows effortlessly from self-realization. This is the cycle which has become the very fabric of my life, and my life's work.

Conscious self-expression applied to writing is an obvious extension of the expertise I've gained from my years of working as a publisher. Despite enjoying international success in my publishing role, and falling in love with the craft of writing along the way, my core passion has always been for the content – the communication of perennial wisdom. Now the primary focus of my work shifts into an ever-deepening relationship with essence, while the accurate and aesthetic nature of form becomes first and foremost the vehicle for its communication.

Paying attention to the deep resonance of the intuitive 'hit' I receive from the words 'Conscious Writing' leads me to purchase the domain name consciouswriting.com as a commitment to future potential.

The wheel is turning, but I know it will take time to complete the commitments that have come from the momentum generated so far. I'm already under way with offering courses, classes and coaching on what I've been describing as 'The Writer's Journey: From Inspiration to Publication'. It's a holistic approach to the nuts and bolts of how to succeed as a published author, and is the content, and the title, of my first book.[1]

This original body of work combines my experience of writing and publishing and offers the inside story for writers aiming to sign a deal with a traditional publisher. I've been developing it since leaving my last in-house position as a publishing consultant for Random House. It's an obvious starting-point in the early days of freedom from corporate life. Yet I sense it's a stepping stone rather than an end in its own right.

Taking the next step leads me to bring the sacred dimension more openly into creativity, writing and conscious living. As I explore ever-deeper levels of inspiration for writing, I find myself launching the International Association of Conscious & Creative Writers (IACCW) in January 2010. The inclination to open the way for writers to 'discover their authentic voice – on the page and in the world' is strong.

Conscious Writing presents itself as the next phase of the emerging vision. I continue to follow the impulse and pick up the trail of resonance as the new content gradually shakes down into a digestible flow that is complete enough to share.

This process results in a one-day Conscious Writing workshop, delivered first online, then live and eventually as a full retreat experience that proves beyond any shadow of doubt to be a powerful approach to deep writing and personal discovery. The impact of the teaching fans the creative embers into radiant flames.

In response to a combination of inner direction and outer request, a decision arises to write a book. Continuing to trust and follow the unfolding dream brings me to this page, this book, through which it is my intention to invite you to taste the Conscious Writing fruit for yourself.

Planting and nurturing the seed of this profound creative process leads to the realization that Conscious Writing is the tip of a vast iceberg.

Above the surface of the water, where 10 per cent of the mighty form is visible for all to see, the benefits show up in tangible terms. Discovering our true voice leads to clarity about our core message, which enables us to write what we are *truly* here to write and express ourselves authentically through all facets of our authorship. Our words shimmer with a vibrancy that invites our readers to feel the depth and impact of our insights and stories at every level.

The 90 per cent of the iceberg that lies below the surface of the water represents all that makes it possible for the 10 per cent to be seen and shared. Herein lie the 'invisibles' of writing that we'll soon explore. This space also contains the potential for internal conscious and creative 'rewiring' to draw all aspects of ourselves into alignment with a sense of wholeness and purpose, and a deep joy that is fuelled by the eternal flame in our heart. Consciously dancing with this essential fire invites the gradual dissolving of accumulated density, ultimately revealing pure light from the core, now liberated to shine equally through silence and through words. Resonating with the same frequency as our soul, we live truthfully, write from our heart and know that it's all a sacred prayer.

As within, so without, and the internal invitation becomes an external invitation as I invite you to dip a toe in the waters of Conscious Writing by working your way through this book. Any degree of sincere immersion makes it possible to discover your true voice and express it authentically on the page and in the world. I invite you to open your mind and your heart and allow the process to work its magic.

Conscious Writing is a way, and a way in, to a whole new level of creative writing and a freedom of being that just is. Turn the page on what has been and let's dive in.

⌣

# INTRODUCTION

Responding to the call of an invitation can be a life-changing experience. It's the first stage on the hero's journey so famously described by the late Joseph Campbell in his book *The Hero with a Thousand Faces*.[1] In this case the invitation arises from within as the hero becomes aware of the 'call to adventure' and, following this inner impulse, undertakes an expedition into the essence of Truth before ultimately returning to take awakened action in the outer world. As we begin our journey into Conscious Writing, my invitation echoes the open nature of this call and paves the way for hidden treasures to rise to the surface and be shaped into appropriate forms, including words. Through aligning ourselves with this natural creative flow, we can ride the wave to previously unexplored realms of infinite potential with full awareness.

Yet the hero may ignore the call to adventure, or even actively resist it. Creators of all kinds know the feeling well. The yearning for creative expression is often blocked – consciously or unconsciously – by some kind of resistance. As we'll soon see, Conscious Writing offers a simple yet profound way around this, just as a mountain stream finds a way to flow around rocks on its way down to the ocean.

In the meantime, by its very nature, an invitation elicits a response: acceptance, rejection or disregard. With acceptance, a whole new world of possibility opens up, and with it, as the hero soon discovers, an array of challenges present themselves before the rewards are revealed.

One of the most important skills to develop to overcome challenges of all kinds is conscious choice. This is the ability to make a decision or choose a course of action from a state of full awareness rather than one of the conditioned responses that largely drive the everyday world.

Conscious choice makes a significant difference to Conscious Writers at every stage of the writing process. We consciously choose to value rather than ignore the first sparks of our ideas. We reorganize the rhythm of our lives in order to show up regularly to write. Ultimately, we commit wholeheartedly to our authorship while honouring our existing commitments.

Starting as we mean to go on, let's consciously choose to remain open to all possibilities as we explore the shallows and depths of Conscious Writing.

## The Overview

Conscious Writing is one form of Conscious Creativity. 'Conscious' points to self-realization and 'creativity' points to self-expression. In the dance of Creation, these naturally flow one into the other as the in-breath and the out-breath of conscious and creative living.

The premise of Conscious Writing is that our state of consciousness determines and shapes the writing we do *and* whether we write – or not, as the case may be. In acknowledging the importance of what we think and feel about ourselves as writers, our ability to write and the value of our work, it reaches into, and beyond, the harmony of head and heart. As we expand the alignment to include all aspects of ourselves and open to what we could call greater awareness beyond our everyday self, we find ourselves approaching writing from a holistic point of view.

The expanded nature of this perspective and the vibrancy we generate by having our body energized, our emotions positive, our mind clear and our attitude open to greater awareness clear the way for deep authentic truth to stir within us. We can see this as our true self, the eternal part of ourselves that lies beyond the conditioning of the everyday self we habitually use to navigate the maelstrom of life. It is from this deep place that our richest and most original ideas arise.

Conscious Creativity harnesses the potential of this whole-self approach to deep inspiration, and Conscious Writing draws on the elegance of words to communicate what we receive. It is an invitation to enter the creative mystery and engage with it consciously. My experience by the wildlife pond is a small illustration of this process in action.

Conscious Writing is essentially about writing from the level of our true self. This requires us to shift beyond our usual identification with our everyday self and put down the intellectual and emotional baggage that most of us carry around without even realizing it.

Beginning our Conscious Writing practice with inner preparation enables us to draw from the well of our true self, which lies beyond the negative thoughts and emotions that often hold us back from realizing our full potential. In the process, we line up the inner true self with the outer everyday self, and this opens a clear pathway for rich creative inspiration to flow freely through us without being blocked or tainted by our everyday anxieties or conditioned mindset.

Poet and author Robert Bly refers to the importance of this alignment when he explains, 'If we want to create art we have to stitch together the inner world and the outer world.'

At this point, we bring in the outer skills of authorship to shape our insights and ideas into language that enables us to communicate the intangible essence in a tangible form which others may benefit from and enjoy. This combination of inner truth and outer expression is a blend of soul and craft, and adds a dimension to our writing that may not always be seen but will always be felt by the reader.

The 'inside-out' approach that Conscious Writing invites us to adopt naturally leads us to discover our true writer's voice. Definitions of the writer's voice usually centre on an author's use of language and style. Yet Conscious Writers are working with additional ingredients that infuse the external forms of language and style with subtle yet distinct qualities that point towards individual *and* universal truth. As we reflect on what it means to discover our true writer's voice from a perspective that includes essence as well as form, we realize that Conscious Writing leads us to a level of communication that is ultimately more alive than the most adept expression of language alone can ever be.

As Conscious Writers, our true essence is expressed through what, and how, we write. Whatever we feel most passionate about sharing is communicated through words that can be woven into any form of writing. Over time, we discover our own unique way of expressing ourselves authentically.

Honing the skills of the writing craft is, of course, fundamental to our success as writers and requires full respect and focused attention. In fact for most writers it is the work of a lifetime and there will always be new levels of aptitude to uncover. There are a multitude of resources available today for acquiring the tools of the trade. Our priority here lies with opening the way for deep and timeless truth to pour through us – onto the page and into the world.

## Going the Extra Mile

Conscious Writing clearly involves more than simply following the impulse to write and capturing brilliant ideas in a well-crafted collection of words. Yet writers around the globe have been doing just that for a long time, and many have achieved impressive success in the eyes of the world. So let's remind ourselves why it's worth going the extra mile and opening consciously to deep inner truth as part of our creative writing practice.

Conscious Writing enables us to discover our true voice and write what we're here to write. Our true voice arises naturally when we're connected with our true self; we release our fears, realize our true purpose and commit to living our truth in the world, as writers and in all areas of our lives. If we feel inspired to make a positive difference in the world, whatever form it may take, in order to succeed we need our writing to trigger the outcomes we want our readers to experience. This is specifically in terms of how they feel at the deepest levels during and after reading our work. Refreshed, uplifted, transformed, joyful and inspired to take action are a few possibilities. Conscious Writing has the potential to transmit a dynamic experience of what Stephen Harrod Buhner so aptly describes in his vibrant book *Ensouling Language* as the 'living reality' beyond, and through, our words.[2]

When it comes to refining the words we've written, Buhner advises us to: 'Work to shape them so that they hold the living reality of the invisibles inside the things you are describing. Once you get to congruency between the writing and the thing itself you will know it, you will feel it.' The vibrancy of this level of writing is likely to remain alive in the hearts and minds of our readers rather than becoming lost as the bedlam of daily life dissolves the clarity we may initially feel from reading anything of significance.

Improving and strengthening the impact of our writing are valuable outcomes of Conscious Writing. If we're also interested in succeeding as published authors, the intimate connection that Conscious Writing has with authenticity enables us to stand out from the myriad other voices clamouring to be heard in the marketplace today.

The polished persona created to be the professional interface between authors and their audience still works for a minority of already well-known writers. Yet there is a strong swing towards authenticity that has been fuelled largely by the opportunity for direct relationships to be built with readers via blogs and social media sites. The digital age is making transparency an increasingly important requirement for success in many areas of the public domain, and there is little to match the charisma of an authentic and passionate author who genuinely walks their talk and communicates with impact.

Interestingly, the more we immerse ourselves in the universal levels of greater awareness, the more distinct we simultaneously become as individuals. This is because what we've learned about who we 'should' be naturally dissolves in the crucible of who we truly are as we blend ever more seamlessly with our true self. As a result, the unique qualities that we alone are able to embody and share in the way that we do become more obvious – to ourselves and to others.

Being clear within this authentic truth naturally attracts people and circumstances that resonate with the truth of who we are and support us on our path. We find people appearing just when we need them or when we set an intention to move in a particular direction. They can be teachers, mentors, agents, publishers, the media and of course readers. Synchronicity becomes commonplace as we find just the right piece of information from a book mentioned in passing by a friend or are introduced to someone who is willing to provide guidance on an area in which we need assistance.

All of this reflects the third and perhaps most important reason why going the extra mile with Conscious Writing is worth every moment of time and attention we give it: it is inherently transformative. As Stephen Harrod Buhner states with succinct precision, 'We are not only the shaper but the shaped.' As we play with the core practices that contribute to deep writing with full awareness, we find the positive effects spilling over and becoming apparent in us as individuals. The inner alchemy clears the way for our authentic light to shine through us in each and every moment, not just when we sit down to write. We feel more alive and aware of ourselves in relationship to our environment and the people who share our world. We become more consistently present to the reality of what 'is' in each and every moment, and experience minimal internal, and external, conflict and judgement. We feel a sense of congruence as we follow the prompting of our heart and understand what it truly means to live in the flow of life itself. Having released the effort of trying to be who we think we *should* be, we discover how easy it is to be who we already are.

With our feet confidently planted on terra firma, we feel grounded enough to reach high above the clouds where clarity reigns, ready to shower us with the fragments and totality of lucid vision. From this clear space we see straight into the core and appreciate the elegance of simplicity. Removing what doesn't serve our purpose becomes a natural part of the process.

We live the balance between focus and flow, and follow intuitive impulses that adeptly guide us forwards in thought, word and deed. Of course, challenges of all kinds still present themselves, yet we tend to handle them more skilfully as we experience the natural ebb and flow of life from a perspective of greater awareness.

Ultimately we reach a default setting of happiness and freedom arising from a distinct sense of connection and wholeness. Conscious living then becomes our highest priority. We set clear intentions to express ourselves consciously and creatively in all areas of life and make the contribution to the world that we're here to make.

## How to Use this Book for Your Conscious Writing Practice

Throughout these pages you'll find an abundance of opportunities to experience all aspects of Conscious Writing for yourself. I invite you to engage wholeheartedly with these principles and practices, which have been designed to guide you to reap the rewards of this holistic approach to deep creative writing.

I encourage you to explore the contents of this book as a living enquiry rather than an exclusively intellectual exercise. This view, combined with appropriate action, will lead you step by step along the path of practice that is laid out in each chapter so you can truly taste the fruit of Conscious Writing.

This graphic ⟿ indicates when it's time to dive in and apply what you've read to your individual situation in order to complement your understanding with personal experience. There are multiple suggestions for writing your results down. You may like to do this in the Conscious Writing Journal that goes with this book (*see page 191*) or simply a blank journal you purchase specifically for this purpose.

All that I teach arises from my own personal and professional learning and experience, which provide the essence as well as the form of everything I've presented here for you. In addition, I've written specifically about my own experience of the content in each chapter, including the challenges I've faced and ultimately overcome, in a section called 'Personal Reflections' (*see page 195*). These lyrical musings can be read before, during or after you explore each topic and dive into your own personal practice. They are a bonus feature complementing each chapter, although they can be skipped if their content and style don't resonate with you.

In the rest of the book:

- In Part I, you'll meet the 'conscious' in Conscious Writing and dive into the greater awareness that lies at the core of our whole approach.

- In Part II, you'll learn how to take forwards the awareness you've cultivated and apply it to nurturing your creative soul.

- In Part III, you'll find the Conscious Writing process, a powerful technique for transitioning into a deep creative space.

- In Part IV, you'll see how everything comes together to create a sustainable Conscious Writing practice.

My suggestion is that you simply start at the beginning and work your way through to the end, especially if you're new to exploring consciousness and creativity.

If you already have some experience of the creative mystery, by all means dive right into the Conscious Writing process in Part III. However, do make sure you have the essential components in place as outlined in Parts I and II if you want to benefit from all that Conscious Writing has to offer. However advanced we are, there are always more levels of refinement to explore in the process of setting ourselves free to create what we're here to create and write what we're here to write.

Finally, you may find that connecting with like-minded Conscious Writers complements your personal understanding and enjoyment of this profoundly creative path and enhances your whole experience of writing and authorship. Guidelines for creating online and offline Conscious Writing Circles for peer-group support, positive accountability and creative encouragement are also included (*on page 192*).

In the meantime, our journey begins with the all-important first step. Are you ready? Let the adventure begin!

# PART I

# Meeting the Conscious in Conscious Writing

# *Who Are You Before the Writing Begins?*

The living enquiry is set in motion with nothing less than the greatest of challenges, to express the inexpressible as we seek clarity on a fundamental question: *Who are you before the writing begins?*

The first shift that Conscious Writing invites us to take is to switch our gaze from its usual outward focus and turn inwards to meet our creative core. Reflecting deeply on this essential question leads us to feel a sense of greater awareness, however faint this may initially be. As part of this process, we come into contact with the 'conscious' in Conscious Writing.

## Dive in

Pause here and dive right in to touch the fringe of the feeling now:

- Close your eyes and take a deep breath in. Exhale for twice as long as you inhale.

- Ask yourself silently, 'Who am I before the writing begins?'

- Release the tendency to grasp for an answer with your mind. Instead, soften your inward focus, imagine your body is hollow and allow the echo of whatever sensation arises in you to be your answer for now. If there is an absence of feeling at this time, accept that without judgement.

- Repeat the question and the self-enquiry with a gentle invitation for clarity to arise within you.

- Continue for as long as it feels right and then stay with it for a little longer to explore ever-deeper layers.

- When you feel ready, open your eyes and jot down a few notes about your experience in your Conscious Writing Journal.

Repeat the enquiry regularly over the next 21 days and pay attention to the subtle sense of awareness that will grow with continued attention and allowing.

The internal question-and-answer dialogue may begin something like this:

Q: Who am I before the writing begins?

A: *I am Alex.*

Q: Who is Alex?

A: *I am a writer/teacher/coach/entrepreneur/practitioner/parent/partner/ friend…*

Q: Who is the Alex who writes…?

A: *I am a human being with a life full of people and projects.*

Q: Who is the human being that has the life full of people and projects?

A: *I am.*

Q: Who is 'I'?

A: *…*

The ultimate answer to the question, *Who am I before the writing begins?* points us towards consciousness itself. Clearly our interpretation of consciousness extends way beyond the regular understanding outlined in the *Oxford Dictionary*, which states that consciousness is simply 'being aware of and responsive to one's surroundings'. Even the additional level included in the *Merriam-Webster* definition 'the upper level of mental life of which the person is aware as contrasted with unconscious processes' remains within narrow boundaries of intellectual understanding.

    With Conscious Writing, we are referring to an appreciation of the totality that the late Indian sage Sri H. W. L. Poonja, or Papaji as he was affectionately known, expresses in his elegant volume *This: Poems and Prose of Dancing Emptiness* as:

*Consciousness.*
*The senses cannot feel It*
*And the mind cannot understand It.*
*Consciousness alone is everywhere*
*And rises as 'I' within you.*[1]

Inspired by the impulse to reach for the living reality beyond words, sages and mystics throughout time have written sacred texts and verses to transmit the essence of consciousness and their direct perception of what it means to be conscious. The opening lines of Lao Tzu's *Tao Te Ching* remind us that 'The Tao that can be told is not the universal Tao. The name that can be named is not the universal name.'[2] Yet reading his words touches something deep within us that resonates with the vastness of the Truth he is revealing.

The word 'conscious' points towards self-realization, and at one level we can understand the basic premise of self-realization as being the process by which we discover an authentic self through psychological and spiritual practices. This is our true self that we increasingly come to recognize as the everyday self releases its grip on our interpretation of who we think we are. Taking the process of self-realization to its natural conclusion leads us to the pure knowledge of who we are beyond our name, the roles we play in life, our physical body and our life story. Ultimately, this leads to the realization that there is no 'self' to realize, which in turn opens us to a direct perception of the true nature of reality.

Internationally renowned spiritual leader the late Sri Chimnoy explains:

> *'Self-realization means self-discovery in the highest sense of the term. One realizes one's oneness with God – consciously.*[3]

As Conscious Writers, we can immerse ourselves as much or as little as we like in the 'conscious' of Conscious Writing. How far down the rabbit hole we go is an individual choice. Yet simply asking the question, *Who am I before the writing begins?* and looking with sincerity for the answers within initiates a response, just as throwing a pebble into a pond can't help but send ripples out across the water.

As with the layers of the proverbial onion, the focus we give to exploring such fundamental questions gradually peels away all that obscures our perception of who we already are. It usually takes time for us to gain a glimpse of the infinity towards which we're directing our gaze. Yet even with a vague sense of something we may not yet be able to articulate, there's a feeling of familiarity, as if we're coming home to ourselves.

Asking who we are before the writing begins and what it means to be conscious is enough to open the door. What we increasingly discover is an awakened state of being which is totally present in the Now and free from the conditioned patterns of thought and behaviour that are a product of the everyday self. This conscious state of being is also naturally creative.

## Seven Core Principles

There are many approaches to becoming and remaining fully conscious. In fact it's a primary focus for all the major spiritual traditions, and despite the differences of expression and methodology, the highest teachings all point in the same direction of perennial wisdom.

Inspired by the golden thread that is consistently found at the core of each tradition, we can draw on seven principles that have specific relevance for the deep approach to writing that Conscious Writing invites us to adopt.

These seven core principles are gateways to the 'conscious' in Conscious Writing and support us to open, and deepen into, conscious awareness. As writers, we can then invite the creative impulse of life itself to pour through us onto the page and experience being the conduit rather than the captain of the vessel.

Arjuna Ardagh expresses this idea using the term 'translucent' in place of 'conscious' in his discussion of art in *The Translucent Revolution*: 'Translucent art does not come from the artist's personal identity, but rather through it. In this sense, all great art is, and always has been, translucent. Vincent van Gogh suffered greatly, yet his paintings, like *Cornfields* or *Sunflowers*, are celebrated as masterpieces not just for their content, but also for the mysterious energy that breathes through them.'[4]

The seven core principles enable us to engage consciously and creatively with this 'mysterious energy' and allow it to breathe through us onto the page. As such, they provide a solid foundation for Conscious Writing and a valuable basis for all aspects of conscious living. The first, and perhaps most important of all, is presence.

CHAPTER 1

# PRESENCE

Simply put, presence is timeless awareness beyond the mind.

When we are present, our view of the world arises from our true self and the mystery beyond, and the everyday self serves as our vehicle of expression. We have a perspective that resonates with vastness and shimmers through us like the sun's rays pouring through the colours of our individual stained-glass window on a bright summer's day. We live the reality of each and every moment and witness thoughts, feelings and reactions without losing ourselves completely in the content of the past or future to which they usually refer. This degree of awareness means that whatever we're doing becomes an end in its own right instead of a stepping stone to an anticipated outcome.

Presence is a quality of being that is the essence of who we are and simultaneously greater than our everyday mind can possibly imagine. It's a paradox, and when we accept the limitations of our capacity to pin down exactly what it is, we set ourselves free to approach it without expecting to grasp it intellectually. As a result, we open the way to experience it directly and recognize what is essentially our natural state of being.

## Dive in

- *Begin by choosing a single point of focus, such as a flower.* Something from the natural world works well. Gaze at it softly with the intention of seeing it in all its glory, using what Henry David Thoreau describes as 'the unworn sides of the eyes', as if you were seeing it for the very first time. Allow feelings of awe and wonder to ripple through you as its colours, shape, texture and scent reveal the miracle of nature.

- *Close your eyes, take a few deep breaths and drop your awareness into your body.* As you sit completely still, send your awareness down the inside of your body to your feet and, without looking, confirm to yourself that your feet are still there. Feel your feet and notice any sensations that verify their presence. Repeat the process with your legs, pelvic area, torso, hands, arms, neck and head, without spending too long on any one area. Then expand your awareness to include your whole body. With practice, you'll be able to feel the energy of life within your entire physical form.

- *Retaining this kinaesthetic awareness of your body, open your eyes and return your gaze to the flower. Now imagine taking an internal step back.* In your mind's eye, perceive the flower as if you were seeing it from the central point between the two hemispheres of your brain, looking out through the lenses of your eyes. This may seem a little strange at first, but with practice your awareness will grow and shifting your perception to this point will become natural. It is from here that a deeper part of you that usually goes unnoticed witnesses the world directly as it is.

- *Stay with the external stillness, internal aliveness and shifted perspective for a few minutes.* When thoughts or feelings arrive, as they will do, avoid being drawn into their content and simply see them as events occurring within your mind. As you release the grip on your regular thought-stream through this self-observation, a subtle shift takes place and you begin to experience awareness beyond thought. Initially this may only be momentary, but as soon as you notice your mind wandering, simply guide your awareness back to your expanded perspective, repeating the above steps as necessary.

- *Finally, allow the feeling of separation between you and the flower to dissolve and write freely about your experience in your Conscious Writing Journal.* At this point, the potential is present for you to discover for yourself the quantum reality that the energy you feel within you is one and the same as the energy of the flower. Writing about your experience grounds the energy and reflects back to your conscious mind the subtle details you may otherwise miss.

This process of expanding our awareness can become an immensely powerful and effective way to transition into the conscious and creative mindset we are aiming for with Conscious Writing.

We start by concentrating on a single point of focus: the flower. Then, through the connection we have with the energy of life within us and the shifted perspective, we develop a degree of absorption where the sense of separation between us and the flower begins to dissolve.

With practice, our awareness naturally continues to expand from the level of absorption to the open awareness beyond thought; that is, presence. Ultimately we come to realize that we already are what we've always been seeking at some deep level within: the way home. In the process, we rediscover that, at our core, we are presence itself.

This is the essence of the non-dual teachings of Advaita, a Sanskrit word meaning 'not two'. Advaita points towards there being one reality which is the very heart of present moment awareness – the essential unity of all that is. One of the most celebrated teachers of Advaita, Nisargadatta Maharaj, puts it like this, 'When you go beyond awareness, there is a state of non-duality in which there is no cognition, only pure being. In the state of non-duality, all separation ceases.'

Of course, all of this exists way beyond logical analysis and intellectual interpretation. It can only be pointed towards in words and *Known* at the primordial level of being that lies within us all, waiting for the right conditions to be realized, just as the flower needs nourishment, water and sunlight in order to open its petals to the world.

Our usual experience of life is through the interplay of opposites – light and dark, subject and object, this and that. Yet fundamentally these opposites dissolve into one complete whole when viewed from the perspective of presence, which involves perception of life exactly as it is, without the interference of concepts, labels and judgements.

The wave cannot be separate from the ocean from which it is formed. On the surface it may appear to be so, but delving into the deep proves otherwise. Expanding our awareness to what lies beyond enables us to know for ourselves the indivisible nature of the primordial state. This is the ocean in relation to our wave of perceived individuality. From here we have direct access to the creative pulse of life itself, and no interference from conditioned patterns of thought or everyday anxieties.

This is why Conscious Writing invites us to engage with the totality of what it means to be present – to invite the creative source to pour through us onto the page and allow our writing to arise from there.

Spiritual teacher and bestselling author of *The Power of Now* Eckhart Tolle likens presence to waiting with total alertness, like a cat waiting in front of a mouse hole intent on catching a mouse. He explains:

> 'In a sense, the state of presence could be compared to waiting. It is a qualitatively different kind of waiting, one that requires your total alertness. Something could happen at any moment, and if you are not absolutely awake, absolutely still, you will miss it. In that state, all your attention is in the Now. There is none left for day-dreaming, thinking, remembering, anticipating. There is no tension in it, no fear, just alert presence. You are present with your whole Being, with every cell of your body. In that state, the "you" that has a past and a future, the personality if you like, is hardly there anymore. And yet nothing of value is lost. You are still essentially yourself. In fact, you are more fully yourself than you were before, or rather it is only now that you are truly yourself.'[1]

## Being Mindful

One of the best-known approaches to being present in the moment is mindfulness. With its origins in ancient spiritual practice, mindfulness was successfully brought into the contemporary western health system as Mindfulness-Based Stress Reduction, or MBSR, by Jon Kabat-Zinn, founding director of the renowned Stress Reduction Clinic at the University of Massachusetts Medical School. He describes mindfulness as 'paying attention in a particular way; on purpose, in the present moment, and non-judgmentally'.

Mindfulness provides a solid starting-point for experiencing presence, as it teaches us to focus completely on every aspect of the one thing we're doing at any one time, without thinking about the past or the future. So we begin by training the mind to be still and rest on a single point of focus. Then, as we've just seen, with practice we expand our focus to experience full awareness beyond the mind as the source out of which the single point of focus – and indeed everything else – arises.

## It's Not Just in Your Mind

Over the last 40 years there have been numerous studies and over 1,000 publications documenting the medical and psychological research on the validity of mindfulness and its many applications for contemporary life. Even the most sceptical among us would be hard pressed to discount the measurable neurological changes that come with the mind-training practices that mindfulness encourages us to adopt.

These changes are brought about through the process of neuroplasticity – our capacity to reshape and rewire our brain. New neural pathways are created and reinforced from thought patterns and behaviours that are either habitually or intentionally repeated.

When we consciously choose to cultivate the states of mind associated with mindfulness, in just a few weeks there are measurable changes in the brain. The number of connections between neurons and the parts of the brain concerned with higher mental processing are noticeably increased, and their related capacities, such as intuitive insight and enhanced creativity, are strengthened.

The tangible benefits of mindfulness echo the value of all good systems of meditation and related practices and contribute directly to the process of Conscious Writing. The more present we are, the richer our experience of writing will be and the more potential our writing will have to make a positive difference in the lives of our readers.

There are a number of practices at the core of mindfulness, which Jon Kabat-Zinn outlines in his many audios and books, including *Full Catastrophe Living*[2] and the more concise *Mindfulness for Beginners*.[3] These include sitting meditation, the body scan, walking meditation and simple yoga postures, all of which are to be found in one form or another in most traditions of spiritual development, as they effectively support us to experience presence.

With any degree of commitment to such practices, we experience the benefits for ourselves. Stilling the chatter of the everyday mind shifts us into creative mode. The parasympathetic nervous system becomes activated, which slows the heart rate, lowers blood pressure and generally calms the body. From here, we are more readily able to notice and release the identification we have with the habitual patterns of thought and behaviour that belong to the everyday self, and as a result show up to write deeply and with full awareness.

As we pay attention, using all our senses to ascertain the reality of what 'is', and sharpen our skills of internal and external observation, we open up the greatly enhanced levels of creativity, clarity and insight that arise from our true self and beyond. Bringing these qualities to the page leads us into rich uncharted waters we would never have discovered were it not for the added dimension of presence.

It's not only our writing that benefits from such increased levels of focus and awareness. These practices enable us to handle the stresses and strains of everyday life in a more skilful manner than might otherwise have been the case. Simply bringing our attention fully into the present moment facilitates clear decision-making, awakened action and an enhanced appreciation of the simple pleasures in life such as drinking a cup of tea. As Vietnamese Buddhist monk, teacher, and author Thich Nhat Hanh suggests, 'Drink your tea slowly and reverently, as if it is the axis on which the whole earth revolves – slowly, evenly, without rushing towards the future. Live the actual moment. Only this moment is life.'

## Stillness Speaks, and Writes

With all of that said, there are of course no absolute requirements, and we can enjoy Conscious Writing at any level we choose. If we don't feel ready for any form of structured practice, or if our current outlook or life situation would make it more difficult than we feel comfortable with right now, we can still take one small step towards presence and benefit greatly from doing so. That one step is to cultivate inner stillness.

Stillness is a simple yet powerful gateway to presence. For Conscious Writers, inner stillness is central because when our mind is perpetually busy with a cacophony of random thoughts, it's all too easy to lose ourselves in that mental activity and become drawn into its content, positive or negative, like a sailing boat whose sails have caught the wind.

This unconscious mental and emotional activity takes us away from, rather than towards, the creative impulse, which has its true source in stillness. We'll learn more about this in Part II. For now, it's sufficient to dip into and appreciate the power of stillness.

In *Stillness Speaks*, Eckhart Tolle once again provides us with a succinct elucidation:

> *'Stillness is your essential nature. What is stillness? The inner space or awareness in which the words on this page are being perceived and become thoughts... When you lose touch with inner stillness, you lose touch with yourself. When you lose touch with yourself, you lose yourself in the world. Your innermost sense of self, of who you are, is inseparable from stillness. This is the I Am that is deeper than name and form.'[4]*

When we apply this to Conscious Writing, we discover that an effective way to write from a present state of awareness is to begin our writing session with a few minutes of conscious stillness.

# Dive in

- Start by settling your body into stillness. Sit comfortably with your back straight, your feet flat on the floor about hip-width apart and your hands resting lightly on your legs with your palms facing down.

- Now bring your attention to inner stillness by closing your eyes to turn your focus inwards and become fully aware of your breathing as the breath flows rhythmically in and out of your body.

- Just feel your breath as it flows in through your nose and notice your lower belly simultaneously expanding. As you exhale, be aware of your belly naturally contracting towards your spine. There's no need to push or strain. You're simply becoming aware of what's already happening.

- Stay with this for about three to five minutes, and each time your mind wanders, gently bring it back to the breath.

- When you feel ready, from whatever degree of inner stillness you've reached, begin your writing.

With practice, this simple yet effective technique that has been taught for thousands of years will settle the chatter of your mind into stillness and enable you to pick up the scent of presence. Ultimately we work towards being fully present in every moment of every day, and from that state of total awareness, engage in conscious thought and awakened actions, including Conscious Writing.

Stillness speaks, and writes.

CHAPTER 2

# ALIGNMENT

The principle of alignment can be approached from a multitude of different directions that all lead to the same point, like the spokes of a wheel meeting in the centre. The methods we choose are less important than the effects they have on how we feel and the clarity of our perception. Certain practices, such as yoga, qi gong and tai chi, have a long history of success with the complete alignment we're aiming for as part of our preparation for Conscious Writing. Yet simply walking with full awareness can lead us to experience the cogs of our creative wheel clicking into place and the way opening for deep inspiration to flow through us and onto the page.

We touched earlier on the premise that our state of consciousness determines and shapes the writing that we do. With Conscious Writing, we reach into and beyond the harmony of head and heart to align every aspect of ourselves with the greater awareness that lies beyond our everyday self. In the process we become congruent at every level and feel a sense of 'rightness', as if we're hitting the mark. It's the feeling of 'yes' at every level of our being.

From here we discover our ability to swim in the uncharted waters of potential and return with inspiration that feels as though it's come from 'elsewhere'. This is how we access the essence of the richest and most original ideas that are shaped into form through the filter of our creative aptitude.

## From the Ground Up

Writers are often lost in thought or caught up in the emotional realm and forget about the importance of the physical body in the creative process. Yet the body is the vehicle through which we express ourselves in the world and it can make an enormous contribution to our creative endeavours.

When we loosen up the body, we create inner space through which creativity can flow. According to psychological research by Leung *et al* (2012), published in the journal *Psychological Science*, people can become more creative simply by changing their physical posture. In one of the studies, Leung had participants explore creative problem-solving using physical movements of their hands to emulate the phrase 'on the one hand ... on the other hand'. Those who gestured with both hands came up with more novel ideas than those who gestured with just one hand.[1]

Learning to synchronize all the aspects of ourselves begins with relaxing and energizing the physical body. Dr Herbert Benson, cardiologist and founder of Harvard's Mind/Body Medical Institute, used the term 'Relaxation Response' to describe a physical state of deep relaxation that engages the parasympathetic nervous system. This is the opposite of the 'fight or flight' response and, as we've already noted, its activation results in a whole range of beneficial characteristics, including muscles becoming less tense and breathing becoming slow and deep, ensuring optimum oxygen intake.

With full relaxation, our brainwaves shift from the everyday beta to alpha and then theta waves, signifying that our mind is alert yet relaxed. In turn we feel calmer and more confident, our concentration, mental clarity and memory improve, and we experience increased levels of productivity during the day.

In addition to the positive results from deep relaxation, energizing the body has the potential to allow access to realms that aren't available to everyday perception. Conscious movement with awareness and intention increases our sensitivity to feel and then optimize the flow of energy within our physical body. Developing this capacity ultimately leads us to sense the underlying energy that science now fully acknowledges lies at the core of everything.

In the search for the source of matter, what scientists actually discovered were increasingly subtle forms of energy, from molecules to atoms, electrons, neutrinos and beyond. Their research confirmed what sages and mystics have been teaching for thousands of years: that the universe, and all it contains, is essentially energy.

Taking this one crucial step further, we discover that energy is in fact the gateway to information. Dr Jude Currivan, cosmologist, author and member of the Evolutionary Leaders' Circle, explains:

> 'Leading-edge 21st-century science is progressively viewing information as being more fundamental than energy and matter, and indeed space and time itself. The reason is that information expressed energetically literally "in-forms" in the sense that it generates manifest forms – through fractal patterns and holographically at all scales and all levels of perception – the realities we experience, and ultimately co-create. Such realities are not only informed and experienced in the physical world, but on individual, archetypal and collective levels in a myriad multi-dimensional realms and altered states of consciousness.'

*∠233_246*

As Conscious Writers, we apply this understanding by learning to develop our energetic awareness to the point where our perception reaches through the surface to the invisible realms beyond. Here we discover the rich creative potential of deep inspiration and intuitive insight directly from the energetic levels of pure information that pour through us onto the page. When we review what we've written, this heightened sense of awareness allows us to *feel* the life of our words as the conduit of content that accurately expresses the living reality towards which they point. This kind of vibrancy is one of the most important criteria for refining and completing our work as Conscious Writers.

# The Heart, the Head and Beyond

### Sophia's Story

*As her 40th birthday approached, Sophia decided that the book she'd thought about writing for so long couldn't be put off any longer. It felt like now or never and she was determined to see it through to completion.*

*As a professional person who had an interest in personal development, Sophia knew all about setting goals and positive thinking. She created a plan and scheduled time in her diary to begin writing.*

*Three months later, with only a few pages of notes written and nothing concrete achieved, she approached me for help. She was dismayed by the fact that despite her best efforts and a strong intellectual determination to write her book, it just wasn't happening. The situation was especially frustrating for her as she was a disciplined person who usually found it easy to stick to her plans. Yet she discovered that sheer willpower didn't work with writing; the harder she pushed, the less progress she made!*

*It wasn't long before the reason for her struggle was revealed. Although Sophia had successfully gathered her thoughts about writing her book, the way she felt about the whole process was entirely different. Deep down she didn't feel that she had anything of value to say, let alone that anyone would be interested in reading her words. Her head and her heart were pulling in opposite directions.*

*Once she became aware of the source of her block, she felt an immediate sense of relief and let go of the enormous pressure she'd been putting herself under. Releasing the feelings of failure and gradually shifting her mindset to draw how she felt into alignment with her intellectual intention to write led to real progress being made at last. She was able to recapture her enthusiasm and her writing started to flow freely.*

Sophia's story isn't an isolated example. When it comes to writing and authorship, our mindset is one of the key factors that makes or breaks our success. The philosopher William James was referring to the power of mindset when he stated, 'The greatest revolution of our generation is the discovery that human beings, by changing the inner attitudes of their minds, can change the outer aspects of their lives.'

With Conscious Writing, aligning what lies deep in our heart with the decisions we make at an intellectual level follows naturally from relaxing and energizing our physical body. Positive attitudes such as appreciation and enjoyment cause neurochemical reactions that assist our brains to operate more efficiently. In fact, actively cultivating a positive mindset actually enhances creativity.

In a study reported in *Scientific American* and published online by the American Psychological Association, J. R. Minkel dispels the myth of depression being the wellspring of creative genius. He describes how psychologists at the University of Toronto induced a happy, sad or neutral state in each of 24 participants by playing them specially chosen musical selections. After each musical interlude, the researchers gave the subjects two tests to assess their creativity and concentration.

In one test, participants in a happy mood were significantly more adept at coming up with a word that unified three other seemingly disparate words. Thinking creatively enabled them to move beyond normal word associations and select more original responses. Minkel quotes psychologist Adam Anderson, co-author of the study, who explains, 'With positive mood, you actually get more access to things you would normally ignore. Instead of looking through a porthole, you have a landscape or panoramic view of the world.'[2]

The results of this and similar studies suggest that a positive mood enables us to be more receptive to information of all kinds and to process and express that information creatively. Of course, that's not to say that we can't write if we're feeling down. However, the quality of writing that comes from that emotional content is distinctly different from that which flows through an open-hearted, happy state of being.

Clearing our everyday emotions creates space for deep insights and ideas to arise in our conscious awareness. One technique that supports this process effectively is journal writing – stream-of-consciousness writing in a journal that is for your eyes only. In fact, 'yin'-style journal writing is one of the core practices of Conscious Writing.

# Dive in

- Approach 'yin'-style journal writing with both focus and flow. The focus is required to show up on a regular basis to do the practice without judgement or any expectation of an end result. Ideally, this will be daily and first thing in the morning (most of the time). The flow or 'yin' style leads us away from a rigid structure or number of pages that have to be completed. Instead, it invites us to develop a more intuitive relationship with the practice based on what is required at the time.

- Write in your journal about anything and everything that's on your mind or in your heart at the time of writing. If you don't know what to write, use that as a prompt and write about not knowing what to write. Allow the writing to pour onto the page freely and ignore grammatical rules, spelling and all but the simplest forms of punctuation. Write until you feel 'done' and know that this practice will clear the space you need for all the other writing that you do, or want to do.

We'll soon see the true significance of having a clear and spacious mind that will allow deeply creative ideas to come to the surface. We'll also point towards the extension of alignment to the greater awareness that is such a critical component of all forms of conscious and creative discovery.

In fact, luminaries such as Albert Einstein, who was well known for prioritizing intuition and imagination in his scientific explorations, have acknowledged the importance of aligning with greater awareness. Einstein said, 'When you examine the lives of the most influential people who have ever walked among us, you discover a thread that winds through them all. They have been aligned first with their spiritual nature and only then with their physical selves.'

We've worked our way towards an understanding of alignment from the ground up, but aligning with the greater awareness of our spiritual nature as a 'top down' approach is equally valid. The choice is ours to make. Either way, complete alignment sets us free.

## Letting Go into Flow

As we saw from Sophia's story, we certainly know when we're *not* in alignment – our writing either doesn't happen at all or, if we force the process, we end up with lifeless words that leave us feeling flat and uninspired.

On the other hand, it's equally obvious when we *are* in complete alignment. When we're aligned, ideas arrive thick and fast at any time of day or night. We pick up fragments that later reveal a picture or receive a vision of the totality in an instant. Either way, words flow freely and we lose all track of time passing. We experience a sense of pure potential as we engage consciously with the creative process. We are in the flow, and the flow pours through us.

The concept of flow was brought to public awareness through the pioneering work of psychologist Mihaly Csikszentmihalyi who became fascinated by artists who got lost in their work. Noted for his work on happiness and creativity, Csikszentmihalyi identified six factors that encompass the experience of flow:

1. Intense and focused concentration on the present moment.

2. Merging of action and awareness.

3. A loss of reflective self-consciousness.

4. A sense of personal control or agency over the situation or activity.

5. A distortion of temporal experience: one's subjective experience of time is altered.

6. Experience of the activity as intrinsically rewarding.[3]

These factors echo many of the core principles of Conscious Writing, although they fall short of leading us to the full conscious and creative potential it offers. Nevertheless, they are helpful indicators in relation to flow and also reflect the role of alignment.

Being in alignment supports us to access flow – *and vice versa*. When we're 'in flow', we're naturally aligned.

One powerful way to trigger writing in flow is to write about what we love and feel most passionate about sharing with others. Following our deepest inner impulse to write what we feel we're here to write creates the right conditions for flow.

In the first instance, however, we may need to let go of what we think we *should* write in order to create space for deep flow and true alignment to occur. Many of us have been consciously or unconsciously influenced by other people in relation to our writing or feel pressure from a part of ourselves to write on a particular topic for a specific reason. Conscious Writing invites us to let these influences go and discover our true calling to write.

## Dive in

- Pause here and ask yourself, 'What influences can I identify relating to my thoughts and feelings about the topic(s) I am considering for my writing?'

- Reflect deeply on this question and write about it freely in your Conscious Writing Journal.

- Be honest if and when you detect any underlying nudges from anyone in your immediate circle, your peer group or a part of yourself that is persuading you to write on a subject because it 'makes sense' to do so.

- Now answer this question: 'What would it take for me to release the feeling that I ought to write on...' (fill in the blank to fit your situation).

- Finally, take action to liberate yourself from any thoughts or feelings of 'ought' and 'should' to clear the way for discovering what truly makes your heart sing. Stream-of-consciousness writing is one effective way of supporting yourself in this process.

CHAPTER 3

# AUTHENTICITY

The more present and aligned we are, the more authentic we naturally become.

True authenticity is about being real at every level of our being, not just at the surface in the manner favoured by reality television. Instead it is about showing up in the world at the level of our true self, which is expressed through the vehicle of our everyday self. It is about speaking, writing, relating to others and living from a deep space of authentic truth. With awareness and practice, this becomes our default setting.

As we develop what can be viewed as a vertical alignment of body, emotions, mind and soul, we discover another orientation in connection with authenticity. This can be described as the horizontal alignment of the inner self with the outer self. Of course these are not entirely accurate as dimensional descriptions of such intangible characteristics, but they do assist us to appreciate the deepest possible interpretation of what authenticity means. Perhaps even more importantly, they help us to *feel* the energy of alignment that strengthens our connection by making the intangible more tangible.

## Releasing and Revealing

When the horizontal pathway between our inner and outer selves is clear, we discover what we are *really* here to write and share with the world. At some level within us, this already exists as pure and timeless potential. Our task is to reveal the essence, which we then shape into congruent forms. Mystical poet William Blake captures this idea beautifully when he says, 'Eternity is in love with the creations of time.' The essence of what we are here to create is timeless, and finds fulfilment through the authentic expression of the words we write and the actions we take in the time-bound world.

Conscious Writing invites us to engage with the deepest levels of authenticity, which require us to release who we think we should be in order to reveal who we truly are. This presents a real challenge for most of us, as the majority of our conditioned patterns of thought and behaviour are deeply ingrained as habitual responses to the stuff of life.

By the time we're adults, we're largely running on autopilot without even realizing it. We've been taught to see the world in a certain way by our parents and peers, and as a result, often follow the path that has been laid out for us. Initially, this may be without even questioning if we're becoming who we think we *should* be and doing what we believe we *ought* to do. It's often only later that we begin to wonder why we don't feel fulfilled. Crises like accidents or health issues, divorce or depression may feel like the end of the world as we know it. Yet in retrospect we may see that they were blessings in disguise, which provided us with an opportunity to reflect on our priorities and review our choices. These turning-point moments also present us with the chance of *conscious* choice with regard to our relationship with true authenticity.

Brené Brown, PhD, research professor, speaker and bestselling author, describes authenticity as 'a collection of choices that we have to make every day. It's about the choice to show up and be real. The choice to be honest. The choice to let our true selves be seen.'[1] Brown is pointing us towards the *conscious* choice of making a commitment to authenticity and reinforcing that choice in *all* the situations and circumstances of our lives.

Allowing ourselves to be authentic to this degree involves completely accepting ourselves for who we are at every shade of every colour of the individual spectrum of our being. It also includes consciously surrendering to Truth and being faithful to inner impulses rather than outer expectations. We need to find the courage to stand firm in the midst of what appears to be a paradox: that we are whole and perfect just as we are, and simultaneously incomplete and replete with imperfection. With the understanding that the former describes our naturally authentic true self and the latter refers to our everyday self, the paradox dissolves and the horizontal alignment of inner and outer becomes an obvious route to genuine authentic expression.

Ralph Waldo Emerson confirms that, 'To be yourself in a world that is constantly trying to make you something else is the greatest accomplishment.' As Conscious Writers, we specifically need to let go of who we think we *ought* to be as authors and what we think we *should* write. Instead, we need to follow our inner calling to write what truly makes our heart sing and share our work with our audience in ways that are authentic to our soul.

## Daring to Be Yourself

Daring to be true to ourselves is also correlated with many aspects of psychological wellbeing, including vitality, self-esteem and coping skills. In fact, acting in accordance with one's core self – a trait called self-determination – is ranked by some experts as one of three basic psychological needs.

A study was done by Michael Kernis and Brian Goldman of Clayton State University.[2] They reviewed a vast array of literature and came up with a bottom-line definition of authenticity as 'the unimpeded operation of one's true or core self in one's daily enterprise'. They also identified four separate components of authenticity that could be measured in a written test:

1. *Self-awareness:* the foremost component, which is also part of the other three and is described as 'knowledge of and trust in one's own motives, emotions, preferences and abilities'.

2. *Clarity:* for evaluating our strengths and weaknesses and acknowledging when we've missed the mark without denial or blame.

3. *Behaviour:* acting in ways that are congruent with our core values even if this carries the risk of rejection or criticism.

4. *Close relationships:* authenticity in the form of honesty and openness is fundamental for intimacy.

The benefits for people who score highly on the authenticity profile as identified by Kernis and Goldman include being more likely to cope effectively and confidently with difficulty, have satisfying relationships, feel a sense of self-worth and purpose and be able to follow through in pursuing goals. These benefits also contribute greatly to our success with writing and authorship.

## Discovering Your Authentic Writer's Voice

Imagine throwing a stone into a still lake and watching the inevitable ripples caressing the surface of the water in ever-expanding circles all the way to the shore. Making a pledge to authenticity has a similar effect in the subtle realms. The ripples that are created with a sustained commitment to inner truth show up in all areas of outer life, including our chosen forms of creative expression.

With Conscious Writing, authenticity opens the way for us to realize our full creative potential as we tap into the deepest sources of inspiration and purpose and follow our inner impulses to their natural conclusion. When we share our work with the world, at whatever level is right for us as individuals, our authentic voice attracts an audience that is drawn to the frequency of the 'ripples' it emits. Readers resonate with us and become loyal to our work through our authentic voice expressed through our words on the page and our presence as authors in the world. Allowing our true voice to be heard is how we stand out from the crowd and make the contribution we're here to make.

Engaging wholeheartedly in the process of discovering our authentic writer's voice is an essential element of successful authorship. Yet clarity around what it is and how to find it can be elusive. The definitions tend to fall into three main categories:

1.  Some people see the writer's voice as the equivalent of an author's style, use of language and development of content, characters and dialogue.

2.  At the next level, it includes the equivalent of the presence an actor has on stage.

3. With Conscious Writing, we take on board all of the above and combine it with the authentic truth of who we are expressed through both content *and* style – what we say *and* how we say it.

Our authentic writer's voice then comes from the inspiration of your true self and is expressed through our expertise as a writer. This gives our writing a timeless quality and over time we develop a voice that becomes recognizable as our own, just like the name we are known by. When someone calls our name, we experience a subtle feeling of 'rightness' that relates to being correctly addressed. In contrast, we experience a more obvious sense of discord if we're called by another name, either in error or in jest. I've never responded well to being called 'Julie' instead of 'Julia' – it just doesn't fit!

A similar scenario applies to recognizing our authentic writer's voice. At first, it may be more apparent when our writing does *not* reflect our innate sense of who we are. We may detect an unconscious pastiche of our favourite author or even a pattern of expression that belongs to our parents, partner or a colleague we admire. The key that unlocks this particular treasure chest, along with similar issues, lies with conscious awareness. With awareness, we gradually release what doesn't resonate with our inner sense of authentic 'rightness' and develop what does.

### Daniel's Story

*Daniel was brought up in an academic family of high-achievers. He was strongly encouraged to see his schoolwork as the most important priority in his life and was actively discouraged from 'wasting time' with frivolous pursuits like creative play. As a bright child, he did exceptionally well at school and went straight on to university, where he successfully completed undergraduate then postgraduate degrees.*

*When he approached me for mentoring support, he wanted to know how to complete the academic book he was writing for his Masters so that it would be the best it could possibly be. This set of criteria wouldn't normally resonate with the level of conscious and creative mentoring*

*I offer, yet intuitively I sensed that there was more going on than was apparent on the surface.*

*In the very first session, a deeper truth started to emerge. Gradually, it became apparent that a significant shift was already under way within Daniel. His requirement to find his writer's voice so that his academic book would exceed all expectations of excellence was the cover for his deep yet previously unacknowledged desire to write authentically from his heart.*

*Initially we worked simultaneously on bringing his existing book project to life and opening the way for him to connect with his true self so that his true authentic voice would be revealed. Over time, he was able to release what he had been taught he should be/do/write and embrace fully the space that had opened up from connecting with his core.*

*Once his academic book was successfully completed, he began a whole new level of his journey, writing from the heart with his authentic writer's voice. In the process, a passion was awakened within him for a topic that he realized was the basis of a mission to which he felt deeply inspired to dedicate himself.*

*This has now become the focal point of his writing and his work, and he is in the process of developing his ideas around it. His writing on this topic will soon be published on a blog and will undoubtedly become a book – and more – when the moment is right. For now, Daniel's desire to write from his heart has taken him to a whole new level of authentic being and consciously chosen creative expression.*

## Create Space for Authenticity

A powerful way to access authenticity that builds on all we have said so far is to cultivate inner space, specifically at the level of our mind, to provide the optimum conditions for authenticity to be present. When the mind is constantly full of random thoughts it becomes like an impenetrable membrane that prevents us from reaching true authenticity. We're unable to reach the level of our true self where the voice of our soul is found. We need to empty the mind to perceive the guiding voice of our inner truth and access the richest levels of our authentic potential.

There is a well-known story of a Zen master who taught this lesson to a learned man who came to him seeking enlightenment. The man had studied for many years and knew a great deal from all of the books he had read. He asked the Zen master to teach him the remaining lessons he had to learn in order to understand Zen and reach enlightenment.

The Zen master suggested they should have their discussion over tea and straight away began preparing it. When the tea was ready to serve, he began pouring it into a cup he had laid out for his visitor. He poured more and more tea into the cup until finally it spilled over the rim, onto the table and then over the edge of the table onto the learned man's robes.

Finally the man cried, 'Stop! The cup is already full and the tea is spilling everywhere!'

The Zen master stopped and gently smiled at him. 'You are like this cup of tea. Your mind is already full and there is no room for anything more to be added. First you need to empty your mind. Then you will know all you need to know.'

There are many versions of this story, but the essence remains unchanged: space is required to know the truth from the level of your true self and to express that truth in the world authentically. Enlightenment could be described as ultimate authenticity.

# Dive in

- One approach to cultivating space in your mind is to become conscious of the space that's already there. Begin by settling yourself into relaxed stillness and deepening your breathing, letting go of any tension in your body on each out-breath.

- Bring your attention to your thoughts. Notice them arising in your mind, and instead of becoming caught in their content, simply let them be, as if you're witnessing them from a distance. They'll soon dissolve if you refrain from feeding them with the energy of your attention.

- Now shift your awareness to the point just after a thought dissolves and before the next one arrives. You'll discover a space here, however brief this may initially be. This is the space of 'no mind'.

- Focus your attention on this space. When you realize your mind has wandered, gently but firmly guide it back to the space.

Stay with this practice for a few minutes at first and gradually lengthen the period of time.

With practice, experiencing the space between your thoughts generates feelings of deep inner spaciousness and peace. In time, the spaces will lengthen and become genuine gateways through which your awareness can pass into the realm of Truth beneath.

Carl Gustav Jung believed that, 'The privilege of a lifetime is to become who you truly are.' As Conscious Writers, we write from there.

CHAPTER 4

# BALANCE

From the perspective of Conscious Writing, balance is understood as the meeting-point between 'heaven' and 'earth' and an expression of the primordial state out of which they arise. This juncture of complementary opposites in the world of duality is an access point to infinite potential yet often remains elusive and only fleetingly experienced.

The natural world is an elegant example of the dynamic nature of balance. Replete with extremes of hot and cold, light and dark, raging and quiescent, it nevertheless has an inherent balance that asserts itself time and again. Through nature we're reminded of the totality where fullness ultimately supersedes disparity.

As individuals, when we're truly balanced, we're consciously connected to the whole through our true self. We're entirely free to make conscious choices about our creative priorities and able to dance with extremes without getting lost in the mists of excess. We can immerse ourselves deeply in inspiration for long periods of time to encourage our creative flow and still retain the capacity to organize and structure the insights we receive. Or we can sharpen our focus to research the best publishing options for our book while continuing to write consciously and creatively.

When we lose our balance, we become entangled in the net of conditioned thought and behaviour that belongs to the everyday self. Without realizing it, we react to internal and external triggers that drive us to live out the conditioned reality we've learned is 'how things are', and often find ourselves on a seesaw of experience we think of as the ups and downs of 'normal life'. As writers, we may experience a free flow of interesting ideas but fail to remember them clearly, or have a multitude of half-finished projects that are never brought to completion. Alternatively, a lack of balance may hold us back from writing at all through a surplus of self-criticism and a paralysing lack of self-belief.

As with all of the core principles, balance is a gateway to becoming and remaining conscious and opening the way for the deepest truth to stir within us and be expressed authentically. Understanding balance at its core will always shift our experience of writing onto a more conscious and productive level.

## The Supreme Ultimate

According to ancient Chinese wisdom, balance comes from the meeting-point of two fundamental energies in the universe, the complementary opposites known as yin and yang:

*Yin:* the feminine, passive energy that is associated with the moon and yields to the forces around it like water flowing around a rock in the middle of a stream.

*Yang:* the masculine, active energy that is associated with the sun and is solid like the rock being sculpted by water into a new form over time.

Together, they give rise to the manifest world in the constantly flowing dance of Creation. These are shown in the *Taijitu*, the 'diagram of the supreme ultimate'.

*Figure 1: The Taijitu*

Often used to signify the balance of opposites, the *taijitu* shows the undifferentiated unity, or primal oneness, as the circle within which the fundamental polarity inherent in the everyday world of duality is seen through yin (black) and yang (white). Each contains the seed of the other, and in creative terms, leads to knowing that every success shows the way to the next level of the process and within every challenge lie new opportunities. This view of the world arising from one indivisible and unchanging whole through the creative interplay of complementary opposites existing in balanced harmony can be found in philosophical understanding and timeless cosmologies.

In ancient Greece, Plato clearly appreciated the nature of the primordial state when he expressed, in his book *Phaedrus*, 'What is on earth is merely the resemblance and shadow of something that is in a higher sphere, a resplendent thing which remains in an unchangeable condition.'

In the Hindu and Tantric traditions, Shakti and Shiva are the two universal forces that symbolize the feminine and masculine principles in eternal union. They are often depicted as two halves of one being with a female and a male side, and they correspond to the two essential aspects of the one divine consciousness. It is through the interplay of these fundamental energies that the world, and all it contains, is in a constant state of dynamic creation. And at the point of intersection, we discover the essence of balance.

True balance in the world of duality points us towards the non-dual nature of the primordial oneness and simultaneously opens the way for us to work consciously with both the passive and the active creative principles. Naturally, *we need both for any kind of successful creative expression*, and when we are balanced, we draw freely on each at appropriate times in the creative process:

- *Yin, the feminine energy* opens our heart and mind to receive the wealth of inspiration and deep insights that lie at the core of Conscious Writing and flow through us onto the page and out to the world.

- *Yang, the masculine energy* provides the focus we need to show up to the page on a regular basis, organize our ideas and express ourselves coherently in a way others will resonate with.

Applying this understanding to the creative process through Conscious Writing, we begin by cultivating the yin, receptive, feminine energy. We turn our attention inwards, invite the deepest levels of truth to *flow* into our conscious awareness and harness the intuitive qualities that will guide our creative expression.

The natural unfolding that follows ultimately leads the yin energy to turn into its complementary opposite, the yang, active, masculine energy. This injection of *focus* enables us to structure our ideas, craft accurate words as congruent forms to communicate our insights and stories, and take systematic action to turn our creative vision into reality.

The vital relationship of these fundamental energies may occur in an instant at the microcosmic level as an idea arises along with the language to express it with ordered clarity. The same principle works at the macrocosmic level, where the overall emphasis of our work shifts from the initial inner flow of first draft writing to the predominantly outer focus we need in order to share our work with others.

As Conscious Writers, we practise inhabiting the space where flow meets focus in the energetic equilibrium that lies at the core of balance. In the process we discover the alchemy that arises from the combination of the essential elements of flow and focus – water and fire respectively.

Applying fire to water creates steam, which symbolizes the result, or fruit, of working with these complementary energies. Through the interplay of focus and flow, the quality of our being and the resulting attributes of our creative expression become increasingly refined at the levels of content *and* the energetic vibration that content emits. Ultimately, this combination attracts those who will benefit from and enjoy our work the most. Our ideal readers are drawn to the frequency of who we are as authors and the ideas we express on the page as well as the actual content our words communicate.

## Finding Balance through Imbalance

In order to find and sustain balance within ourselves as Conscious Writers, first we need to appreciate the dynamic quality of balance itself. We don't discover balance and bask effortlessly in its glow ever after. Maintaining it requires an ongoing commitment of subtle moment-to-moment awareness – hence its role in supporting us in becoming and remaining conscious.

Paying attention to where we are in relation to balance as part of the Conscious Writing process allows us to fine-tune our experience and make adjustments quickly whenever they are required. In this way, we largely avoid the most extreme reactions of thought and emotion, or at least manage to dissolve their grip on us after a fleeting foray into radical realms.

With this understanding in place, one effective way to map our route to balance is to identify where we're out of balance and then take conscious action to redress the imbalance through immersion in the energy that we identify as lacking.

When we reach a point of equilibrium, it feels effortless and free, like finally learning to ride a bicycle after the early struggle with stabilizers. We enjoy open access to the deep creative flow we need to do our work and feel confident that even if we aren't yet able to see the big picture, clarity will come as long as we continue to take small steps on a regular basis.

As Conscious Writers, we receive many clues that indicate we're out of balance. Drawing on the Taoist terminology and picking up the thread of earlier examples, if we have too much yin and not enough yang energy in relation to our creative writing, we're likely to feel inspired by an abundance of ideas but struggle to coordinate ourselves and structure our thoughts coherently. We may have snippets scribbled on scraps of paper but no idea where the fabulous insight that came to us just yesterday might be!

Alternatively, if we have too much yang and not enough yin energy, we may be wonderfully organized with all of our notes neatly filed and a sophisticated writing schedule adorning our wall. We may show up regularly to write, only to realize that our writing is flat, forced and uninspired. When writing feels like something we *have* to do rather than something we *want* to do, it's time to pause and, as a first port of call, review our relationship with balance.

## Dive in

Identify your current relationship with balance:

- Reflect on where there might be imbalance for you in relation to your writing and authorship, and write about it in your journal. Be honest about your usual habits and tendencies, and realistic about your current situation.

- Identify at least one action you will take to introduce more of the energy you need to restore your balance and make a commitment to your chosen action(s) for a minimum of 21 days. For example:

  → *If you have too much yin and not enough yang energy*, commit to inviting more yang focus into your creative life through sorting yourself and your ideas out to whatever degree is possible at the present time. You could create a writing schedule for example, or engage in short bursts of fast writing for just 15 minutes at a time to build 'heat' and momentum into your writing experience.

  → *If you have too much yang and not enough yin energy*, commit to inviting more yin flow into your creative life by focusing on nurturing your inspiration through nature, music and the company of like-minded creative writers (*see page 188 for more on this*). Concentrate on reigniting your creative fire and connecting more deeply with the intuitive flow of first draft writing.

Be creative with the possibilities for redressing the imbalances you discover and strengthen your commitment by writing about your experience of the actions you are taking daily in your Conscious Writing Journal. It all counts as part of the Conscious Writing process.

## Right Brain, Left Brain, Whole Brain

One final level of insight in relation to appreciating the contribution balance can make to us as Conscious Writers comes from contemporary research into the neuroscience of creativity.

It's a common misconception that creative flow is primarily a function of the right hemisphere of the brain while analytical focus is governed by the left hemisphere. This view dates back to the 1960s, when Roger W. Sperry, who received the Nobel Prize in 1981, studied the effects of epilepsy. He discovered that patients who underwent a surgical procedure to cut the *corpus callosum* (which connects the two hemispheres of the brain) experienced fewer seizures.

Along with other researchers, Sperry carried out a number of studies that identified which parts of these patients' brains were involved in language, drawing and other functions. Some of the results indicated that the right hemisphere was generally stimulated through activities requiring more holistic perception and the left hemisphere was generally stimulated through activities requiring more analytical thinking. These findings then became increasingly over-simplified as their popularity grew, to the point where many people now believe that the right hemisphere of the brain is the source of imagination and intuition and the left hemisphere is associated with language and logic.

Psychologist and bestselling author Daniel Goleman, PhD, has described this misunderstanding as 'outdated neuromythology', and the latest findings from research into the neuroscience of creativity clearly indicate that creativity is a product of the whole brain. Goleman explains, 'The new understanding about left and right hemispheres is more specific to the topography of the brain: when it comes to left versus right, do you mean left front, left middle, left rear? We now understand that when it comes to creativity it's not just left–right, it's also up–down – it's the whole brain.'[1]

The most recent studies also indicate that different regions of the brain are used according to the specific creative task we're undertaking. Developing ideas, for example, won't draw on the same areas of our brain as editing the first draft of our manuscript or writing a press release to promote the forthcoming publication of our new book.

Interestingly, a number of brain regions work together and enlist structures from both right and left hemispheres, creating networks that are particular to the requirements of the task at hand. Cognitive psychologist and author Scott Barry Kaufman identifies three large-scale brain networks in relation to the neuroscience of creativity:

1. The Executive Attention Network for laser-focused attention.

2. The Imagination Network (also referred to as 'the Default Network' by Randy Buckner) for 'constructing dynamic mental simulations based on personal past experiences such as used during remembering, thinking about the future, and generally when imagining alternative perspectives and scenarios to the present'.

3. The Salience Network, which enables switching between networks through regular checking of external events and the internal stream of consciousness.[2]

A great deal more research is required to understand the details of these complex processes. Yet it is already clear that the creative process is a product of the whole brain rather than being governed primarily by one hemisphere alone.

These neuroscientific discoveries elegantly echo the teachings of the ancients, which have pointed us right from the start towards the undifferentiated whole, the creative source out of which everything pours and into which everything ultimately returns. This view encourages and empowers us to adopt a whole-brain holistic approach to all aspects of authorship in the knowledge that this is how we will harness our greatest potential and achieve our greatest success, whatever that means for us as individuals.

From here we naturally prioritize balance as the foundation from which we confidently integrate our ability to express ourselves creatively with the aptitude we need to do so fruitfully. When we engage with the two primary forces of nature from a point of balance, we create what we're here to create and write what we're here to write. Finally we release all effort and allow the natural unfolding to guide the stream of our creative endeavours back to the ocean of potential and witness the effects that arise from this central cause.

# CHAPTER 5

# SIMPLICITY

From the perspective of our true self, in present moment awareness, everything is gloriously simple. It just is.

Free from fears and cravings, we see what's truly important rising effortlessly to the surface. Everything else self-liberates as phenomena occur and then naturally dissolves when we learn to let the small stuff be. Layers of distraction are washed away as we surface from the story, clear of the baggage the everyday self adores, which usually keeps us submerged in endless clutter and unnecessary complication.

A commitment to simplicity supports us in creating space for our true self to become our default setting. From here we clear the path to our chosen priorities and relish the delight of simple pleasures such as the exquisite aroma of freshly ground coffee, celestial art created by clouds and time alone reading an absorbing book. With less, we appreciate more.

Aristotle reminds us that, 'Nature operates in the shortest way possible.' Complexity in the natural world wastes energy. We know from our own experience just how exhausting it is to sift through the overwhelming outpouring of everyday information and to chase the mythical end of the ever-expanding 'To Do' list.

Valuing simplicity has a long history. Almost 2,500 years ago, Confucius declared, 'Life is really simple, but we insist on making it complicated.' All of the major spiritual traditions and world religions teach their own version of material moderation and spiritual abundance. It's not so much that material possessions or financial abundance are the 'root of all evil' – it's our attachment to them that triggers the ultimately suffocating desire of always wanting *more*.

Bhutan may be one of the poorest nations in the world, but with Buddhism as the main religion, it ranks as one of the happiest and measures the wellbeing of its people by Gross National Happiness (GNH) rather than Gross Domestic Product (GDP). The Bhutanese seem to be living the truth of Lao Tzu's maxim: 'He who knows he has enough is rich.'

Zen, a school of Mahayana Buddhism, favours the simplicity of direct insight, understanding and experience. It has drawn countless students from East and West into the deepest appreciation of its simple yet profound philosophy. Zen points us towards realizing the true nature of reality and taking awakened action – right here, right now.

Entrepreneur, inventor and co-founder of Apple Inc., the late Steve Jobs, was drawn to Buddhism at an early age and applied Zen simplicity to his ground-breaking designs. Simplicity was one of his core mantras. He famously stated, 'The way we're running the company, the product design, the advertising, it all comes down to this: Let's make it simple. Really simple … Simple can be harder than complex. You have to work hard to get your thinking clean to make it simple. But it's worth it in the end because once you get there, you can move mountains.'

Simplicity isn't just a pillar of Zen Buddhism. It's also recognized more widely as a way of living that Duane Elgin, author of the classic book *Voluntary Simplicity*, describes as 'outwardly simple and inwardly rich'. With less focus on materialistic consumption and the actions required to pursue those conditioned desires, we've more freedom to enrich our lives with consciously chosen priorities such as spiritual exploration, spending more time with loved ones and undertaking creative pursuits like writing.

Science also pays attention to the power of simplicity through the principle of Occam's Razor. Attributed to the 14th-century logician and Franciscan friar William of Ockham, this states that 'Entities should not be multiplied unnecessarily.' In other words, when all things are equal, the simplest theory is the most likely to be true.

Of course many great writers have praised the value of simplicity, including Shakespeare, who stated that 'Brevity is the essence of beauty.' Two of the great Transcendentalists of the mid-19th century, Ralph Waldo Emerson and Henry David Thoreau, believed wholeheartedly in simplicity, and Thoreau affirmed, 'Our lives are frittered away by detail … simplify, simplify.' Prioritizing a connection with nature, both Emerson and Thoreau felt that simplicity enabled us to encounter the deepest potential of our soul and enrich the farthest corners of our imagination. Their outstanding creative output based on this view speaks for itself.

## What Makes Your Heart Sing?

Simplicity does not equate with sacrifice and living 'without'. In fact it is about living a richer life from enjoying an abundance of all that we feel in our heart of hearts is *truly* important to us. As Conscious Writers, that includes time and space to connect with our core, nurture our inspiration and write what we're here to write. It's easy to become habitually busy, but are we just shuffling papers and drowning in admin, instead of engaging with what's crucial for our conscious and creative fulfilment and expression?

To realize the joy of simplicity for ourselves:

1.  First we need to identify what is essential for us to feel a profound sense of freedom and wellbeing and to know what genuinely makes our heart sing.

2.  Then we need to recognize what lies in the way of experiencing a life that includes our consciously chosen priorities.

3.  The next step requires us to take action to clear the inner and outer obstacles and distractions that lie between us and the essentials we've named.

4.  Finally, we need to value the space we've created so highly that we avoid being drawn into old habits and finding ourselves back where we started, drowning in endless clutter.

Over the last few years, blogger and author Leo Babauta has written extensively on simplicity and gained a following of over a million readers in the process. He describes his work on Zen Habits, now one of the top 25 blogs and top 50 websites in the world, as being about 'finding simplicity in the daily chaos of our lives ... clearing the clutter so we can focus on what's important, create something amazing, find happiness'. He expands on the process of realizing the joy of simplicity in a multitude of articles, all grounded in his personal experience of 'walking his talk' over the last 10 years.[1]

What stands out from what he writes as an echo of all that we're discussing here is that experiencing the value of simplicity usually requires a shift in our mindset. This may be triggered by reaching the end of our tether with the chaos of everyday life and the constant fire-fighting required to find any time and energy for ourselves, let alone our writing.

The leap to a new way of thinking and feeling may also arise from a deep recognition that life is short and unpredictable. We may ask ourselves, 'If I'm not happy and creatively fulfilled now, when will I be? What do I need to do for that to become my reality? When am I going to start/complete the book I've been thinking about for so long?'

All successful mindset shifts require us to find the courage to embrace change. As Conscious Writers, working from the inside out, we peel away the layers of all that obscures our impulse to write. Then we find our own solution for dissolving the disruptions to our intention to do so.

Making a commitment to simplicity is an ongoing process that takes time to implement but gathers momentum and showers us with cumulative benefits. As Conscious Writers, simplicity leads us across multiple thresholds towards increasing clarity and ease with our ability to express the essence of our message on the page. And it all starts with identifying what makes our heart sing.

# Dive in

Pause here for a while and reflect on these two related questions:

1. *'What makes my heart sing?'* Apply this to the big-picture perspective of your whole life and all it currently contains.

2. *'What makes my heart sing as a writer?'* Apply this to your ideas for writing and authorship.

Play with some of the following possibilities for deeper exploration:

- Gaze softly out of the window and allow the fruit of your reflections to take shape gradually rather than grasping for the 'answers' with your mind.

  → Imagine wisps of white steam dancing against a dark background and slowly forming into a symbolic shape you recognize as a clue to the clarity you seek.

  → Or listen with your inner ear to the sounds of words or phrases as they arrive in your awareness, and tune yourself in to the ones that have the deepest resonance for you at this time.

- Turn a blank sheet of paper sideways (landscape) and in the middle write: 'My Life.'

  → Brainstorm all of the existing components of your life and write these on your page, connected by a network of lines to the central point and unfolding from there according to relatedness, in the form of a mind map.

  → Use a coloured highlighter pen to identify what stands out from the page when you look over your mind map with the 'What makes my heart sing?' question in the back of your mind.

  → Choose a different coloured pen to highlight what stands in the way of experiencing more of your chosen priorities.

  → Write up the results in your Conscious Writing Journal. Then add three actions you will take in the next week to free yourself from the obstacles you've identified and move closer to living a life that inspires your heart to sing out loud!

- Repeat the mind-map process with 'My Writing' at the centre of your page and brainstorm all of the ideas you currently have for your writing.

- Write in your journal about each area you identify as being important to you and let the writing itself show you, through ease, abundance and vibrancy, where your sacred heart's desire truly lies.

Carry the question, *What makes my heart sing?* forwards as a living enquiry for as long as you need to discover what resonates most with your core. Remember that your selections only have to feel *right enough for now*. Be prepared to let go of all that you have outgrown, simplify your choices to immediate priorities and create a folder of future possibilities to return to when you are ready.

Even more importantly, realize that you're free to write what makes *your* heart sing – not what you think or feel you *should* be writing as dictated by your intellect, pressure from your peers or even well-meaning friends and family. Simplicity sets you free to make your own decisions and, as a Conscious Writer, follow the inner impulse of your soul's calling to write what you're here to write.

Of course, none of this is set in stone. You can revisit the process and revise your priorities as your awareness increases and your journey unfolds.

## The Elegance of Essence

Italian sculptor Michelangelo knew a great deal about stone, among his many other talents as a painter, poet, architect and engineer. When asked about carving the statue of David, he explained that it was simply a case of removing the stone that didn't look like David.

This creative perspective reveals the core of simplicity as a Conscious Writing principle. It's about focusing on the essence of our message and removing what we don't need to disclose while keeping precisely what we do need to serve our purpose effectively. Antoine de Saint-Exupéry, author of *The Little Prince*, expressed the elegance of simplicity when he stated that, 'Perfection is achieved not when there is nothing more to add but when there is nothing more to take away.'

The irony of writing a whole chapter on simplicity is evident when it could be said that one word would suffice as a call to action: 'Simplify!' Yet arriving at an appreciation of simplicity that has any chance of duration requires a multi-faceted approach to break through our habitual tendency to operate in the jungles of complexity.

As Conscious Writers, we initially invite the full extent of insight and ideas to pour through us onto the page as we create the first draft of our work. Then we release our attachment and, with fresh eyes, embrace the refining and revising of the editing process with creative enthusiasm. Ultimately, we're feeling our way forwards to a 'less is more' outcome.

Simplicity invites us to do more with less. This involves a greater degree of imagination and creativity. As Mark Twain remarked, 'I didn't have time to write a short letter, so I wrote a long one instead.'

Finding the balance between the skeleton writing of extreme staccato style and an over-written excess of words is a personal matter of preference and style. The essence of our message still requires heart and soul to sing a song our readers will take pleasure in. Yet the elegance of simplicity sharpens our focus as we remember that we don't have to write everything we know in our current project. A future possibilities file is a fantastic repository for whatever isn't directly necessary for our readers to feel the truth of what we're sharing.

When all is said and done, Conscious Writing encourages us to carve our own path and benefit from applying universal principles to our individual situation. Here are three final tips to support you in maintaining an ongoing commitment to simplicity as a work-in-progress.

Simplify your:

- outer environment by clearing the clutter and creating a space to write that only includes what you absolutely need

- inner environment with regular stillness and silence to quiet the chatter of your everyday mind

- writing process by taking small steps on a regular basis in the knowledge that every book is written one word, one paragraph, one section at a time.

Slowing down to savour the simple pleasure of writing and letting go of multi-tasking once and for all will enhance our experience as Conscious Writers, as well as the end results of our creative endeavours. As Jack Kerouac summed up so well, 'One day I will find the right words, and they will be simple.'

# CHAPTER 6

# INTUITION

Before the technical revolution began the process of redrafting the landscape, I learned the business of publishing from the ground up. Inspired by the mission of communicating perennial wisdom to a contemporary international audience, I quickly realized that commissioning books for publication was more of an art than a science. This was especially the case in the world of independent publishing, where breaking new ground and working at the cutting edge were the norm.

I hadn't planned to develop my intuition as part of my work. Yet it wasn't long before I experienced the limitations of decisions made on facts and figures alone. Introducing timeless knowledge to a rapidly developing marketplace required greater insight than the study of past success provided. Add to that the publishing reality of working one or two years ahead of the moment readers would discover the end results in printed form, and it became clear that a 'sixth sense' would be extremely valuable.

Looking back, I now see that making a conscious choice to develop my intuition at an early stage of my publishing career was the difference that made the difference – not just to my work, but to all areas of my life. In fact, the opportunity to combine my intuitive hunches with the available information to make whole-mind decisions became one of the aspects of publishing I enjoyed the most.

Of course, we didn't get it right all of the time. Yet over the years the successes outweighed the failures, and in the process my intuition became increasingly accurate. Today, intuition is an integral part of who I am and how

I live my life. It stands out as a defining feature of my work and has become my most trusted ally.

## Looking Inside

Intuition comes from a specific kind of inner perception that the Latin origin of the word points towards: the verb *intueri* means 'to look inside' or 'to contemplate'.[1]

Intuition is a distinct sense of direct Knowing that transcends the use of intellectual reasoning. It arises from beyond our conscious awareness and delivers immediate insight that we aren't able to pin down to the rational thought and logical justification of the everyday mind. In fact, medical researcher and virologist Jonas Salk, who developed the first successful inactivated polio vaccine, identified that 'intuition will tell the thinking mind where to look next'.

Regular perception is based on the identification and interpretation of sensory information. The five senses that most of us are familiar with – sight, sound, taste, touch and smell – send signals to be processed in the nervous system. This enables us to make sense of our environment and function effectively in everyday life.

This level of perception is also strongly shaped by our attention, expectations, motivation and memory of past experience. In fact, the brain's perceptual systems have now been shown to 'actively and pre-consciously attempt to make sense of their input'.[2] In effect, the maxim 'Believe it and you will see it' is far more accurate than most people realize.

Many researchers include intuition in this category of perception that relies on past experience and knowledge. In a world where certainty doesn't exist, hunches or gut feelings are seen to contribute significantly to many of the major decisions we make in life, yet are labelled as emotion-based learning. Author and Science Channel contributor Garth Sundem explains, 'Based on the emotional significance of past events, you learn to approach or avoid similar situations in the future – without needing to process these situations consciously.'[3] Women's intuition is often dismissed as an enhanced ability to read other people's emotions.

However, the narrow definition of intuition as emotion-based learning falls short of explaining the documented success of those who have developed their intuitive abilities to a high degree.

Medical intuitive Caroline Myss, PhD, is a pioneer in the field of energy medicine, a five-time *New York Times* bestselling author and internationally renowned speaker who specializes in the fields of consciousness and health and the science of medical intuition. She has worked extensively with C. Norman Shealy, MD, PhD, a Harvard-trained neurosurgeon and one of the world's leading experts in pain management, founder of the American Holistic Medical Association and co-founder, with Caroline, of the American Board for Scientific Medical Intuition. With her own educational institute, CMED, a raft of seminal research and a multitude of media and teaching activities under her belt, Caroline has forged an impressive path at the intersection of science and spirituality.

Caroline has a verified accuracy rate of 93 per cent in relation to her diagnosis of diverse medical conditions. She developed her aptitude from performing over 10,000 readings over a 12-year period, which were all validated by mainstream medicine under the medical supervision of Dr Shealy. She describes medical intuition as:

> *'...an energetic skill ... [which] operates according to*
> *mystical laws. There is still cause and effect, but mystical*
> *laws operate without the factors of time and space...*
> *Intuition is a higher functioning energetic sense... A medical*
> *intuitive must know how to read symbolic language,*
> *impressions that come at the speed of light – energy*
> *information does that. An intuitive discerns what the*
> *information represents in relation to the person's health and*
> *the root of illness ... the history and story that this energetic*
> *information is telling through the body.'*[4]

Medical diagnosis is just one area where intuition has already proven its worth. Many pioneers from all walks of life, including Albert Einstein, Carl Jung and Bill Gates, have openly commented on the contribution intuition has made to their innovative work.

Intuition is definitely gaining credibility in the fields of scientific research, business development and creative discovery. However, if we want to experience the full potential of this powerful and latent ability we all have, we need to shift our thinking beyond the boundaries of our current expectations. As Einstein summed up so well, 'The intuitive mind is a sacred gift and the rational mind is a faithful servant. We have created a society that honours the servant and has forgotten the gift.'

## Discovering Golden Threads

Intuition has long been associated with creativity and writing, but isn't always labelled as such. The poet William Stafford developed the concept of golden threads, inspired by William Blake's original 'golden strings' from his poem:

> *I give you the end of a golden string*
> *Only wind it into a ball,*
> *It will lead you in at Heaven's gate*
> *Built in Jerusalem's wall.*[5]

Stephen Harrod Buhner takes us on an inspiring tour through Stafford's understanding of golden threads in his book *Ensouling Language.* He explains how we find and follow the golden threads of inspiration by focusing on the *feeling* we have for something that sparks our interest.

As writers, we start by turning our full attention towards the essence of whatever we've noticed and then tease out the essence in the form of words. Once we've captured the initial impulse, our thoughts, seemingly of their own accord, are drawn to something else, and then something else. We pursue the unfolding process and gradually a thread emerges that connects what appear at first sight to be unrelated things. We follow that golden thread wherever it leads, and are careful not to manipulate the direction it takes based on some pre-ordained idea of where it *should* end up. Eventually a complete picture emerges from the disparate components we've explored as part of our golden thread experience and we *Know* we've arrived.

Essentially, this is an alternative way of describing how to follow our intuition, and as Lao Tzu advised more than 2,000 years ago, 'A good artist lets his intuition lead him wherever it wants.'

## Nudges from Creativity

Intuition serves us well as Conscious Writers. The hunches we feel are like nudges from creativity itself. When we pay attention to these deep inner signals, we're brought to writing what we're here to write.

Intuition guides us to select the ideas to focus on from the plethora of possibilities that are often part of the mix. It alerts us to future potential with strong feelings about specifics, just like the intuitive 'hit' I received when the words 'Conscious Writing' originally flooded into my awareness. I knew that purchasing the URL was a commitment I needed to make immediately, even though it was clear that I wouldn't be able to take action to develop the detail for a while.

When we apply intuition to creative writing, it's like signing up to go on an adventure into uncharted territory without a map and trusting our inner resources to lead us where we need to go. The more we trust, the deeper we go, and the richer the rewards in the form of sparkling insights and innovative angles from which to view otherwise hidden facets of our subject or story.

The fresh perspective is the sieve through which the nuggets of gold rise to the surface and find their way to the page. Once there, intuition allows us to *feel* the resonance of each word in relation to the rest, and the difference it makes to reorder a sentence, a section or the whole book. Intuitively, we sense the rhythm and flow and impact of our writing as it pours across the page on its way to sharing what we're here to share.

Writing that is intuitively inspired will always deliver deeper, richer and more meaningful content than that produced by the everyday mind and emotions. And it doesn't stop there. As Conscious Writers, we draw on intuition at every stage of the creative process as we take our work out to the world. It steers us towards the right people to work with – editors, designers, printers, agents, publishers – and the most rewarding route to providing our readers with abundant access to the results of the creation that has flowed through us.

Of course this isn't in isolation of the facts and figures we need to make educated choices at critical stages along our publishing path. It is *as well as* the regular information required to review our options and make whole-mind decisions in service of the ultimate purpose of our Conscious Writing.

## It's Just a Hunch – or Is It?

We've all had experience of intuitive impulses, gut feelings or unexplained hunches that have proven to be correct. Think about times when you've found yourself saying, 'I just had a feeling you would call,' when a friend phones you out of the blue.

You might remember feeling that something wasn't quite right about a situation without being able to pin down exactly why, only to discover that the possibility you were considering wouldn't have worked for you at all.

Or you may have required an insight for a creative task or writing challenge of which you had no previous experience. Your hunch about the best way to move it forwards later proved to be the perfect solution, yet you had no idea how you came up with it.

## Dive in

- Take a few minutes now to cast your mind back over your own experience of intuitive whispers.

- Think about instances where you've had a feeling about something or someone or a specific situation that later proved to be correct.

- Nudge yourself beyond thinking that this hasn't happened to you. It almost certainly has. You just need to stretch your memory to recall instances you may have originally dismissed as chance.

- Identify at least three occurrences, however small, when something beyond your rational mind has been at work, and write about them in your Conscious Writing Journal.

- Aim to add three more over the next three weeks to train yourself to be open and notice when these instances occur.

Unfortunately, most of us have been taught to trust intellectual analysis and rational thought exclusively. At best, we probably haven't received any encouragement to develop our intuition. At worst, we may have been actively discouraged from paying attention to anything other than scientifically verified facts.

As a result, we tend to dismiss our intuitive whispers with rationalizations like 'It's just a hunch' or 'Just coincidence.' Yet ignoring the 'still, small voice' or purposefully disregarding what could provide us with immensely valuable insight is like walking away from an open door inviting us to experience new levels of perception. Conscious Writing leads us across the threshold towards an intuitive awareness that pushes the boundaries of regular creativity and integrates our ability to see simultaneously the complete picture and the most intricate detail.

# Developing Your Intuition

## 1. Pay Attention

The first step across the threshold of intuitive perception involves learning to recognize the way our intuition already makes itself known to us – or would do if only we'd pay attention!

People experience intuition differently. For me, it's a distinct sense of whole-body *Knowing* that I've come to trust unconditionally. Other people experience visual, auditory and/or kinaesthetic impressions. Yet underpinning all of these variations lies a *feeling* that we come to recognize as an indicator of intuition at work. Once again Einstein corroborates and sums up by saying, 'I believe in intuitions and inspirations. I sometimes *feel* that I am right. I do not *know* that I am right.'

Intuitive feelings are often located in specific parts of our body. The well-known 'gut instincts', for example, show that many people feel intuitive hunches in their belly. This isn't to be confused with the 'butterflies' we feel before a performance or presentation. The best way to become skilled at differentiating between the two is through practice and experience. The more we pay attention to our intuitive hunches and how they show up for us, the more we notice them and the more useful they become.

As we expand our awareness, we realize that intuitive insights come to us in a multitude of ways, including through our dreams. We may also notice more subtle details in the world around us. Paulo Coelho tells the story of how Santiago learned to 'read the signs of the world' in his bestselling fable *The Alchemist*.[6] We can learn to do the same.

As Conscious Writers, when we pay attention to our intuition, we may receive flashes of insight simply from seeing a particular shape in the clouds. Hidden messages may be revealed through our stream-of-consciousness journal writing, or we may follow a hunch and discover precisely the information we need for the next section of our book.

## 2. Listen Consciously

Paying attention develops awareness that we can enhance further with Conscious Listening. If we want to hear what is often described as the 'still, small voice' of our intuition, we need to quiet the constant chatter of our everyday mind and be present and alert to the whispers and subtle sensations we're receiving.

Conscious Listening includes both inner and outer focus:

- *Outer listening* involves taking note of the world around us with curiosity about life, people and relationships, all of which provide potential inspiration for our writing.

- *Inner listening* involves turning our focus inwards to what is going on deep inside us – the sounds and the silence, the sensations and the stillness, all of which lie beyond the stories our everyday mind loves to create and replay over and over.

When we listen consciously, we may not actually hear anything we recognize at the time. However, later that day an idea, image or phrase may pop into our conscious awareness and be a whisper from our true self, which has found its way through to us from the opening we created through Conscious Listening.

The following practice can be done at any time but is especially useful if you're wrestling with an issue relating to your writing and churning possibilities over in your mind but not finding the clarity you seek.

# Dive in

- Set aside some time to close your eyes, relax your body, deepen your breath and turn your attention to listening consciously.

- Encourage the whirlwind of your thoughts to settle and stay focused on simply listening. First listen to the sounds around you and then withdraw your attention to your inner space.

- Be patient and simply abide in the alertness of listening, initially for just a few minutes and for longer as your capacity increases.

- If an insight or idea arises, write it down at the end of your Conscious Listening practice.

- If not, that's absolutely fine. Remember that the value of your practice may reveal itself at a later stage, so remain alert in the hours and days afterwards.

Sufi mystic Hazrat Inayat Khan commented, 'My intuition never fails me, it is I who fail when I do not listen to it.'

## 3. Practise, Trust and Follow Through

With everything in life, when we learn something new we develop our skills through practice, which ultimately leads to mastery. So, accessing intuition freely comes through practice – and plenty of it. Yet the subtleties of our sixth sense truly begin to show their colours when we develop the capacity to trust our intuitive impulses and then act on them. The resonance I felt in my publishing days when assessing a project for publication would have amounted to nothing had I not been prepared to trust my intuition. From there I needed to back up my feeling with whatever information was to hand and then take action to see the project through the publishing process.

As Conscious Writers, we can build up our intuitive abilities by following our inner impulses about what topic to write on and which people to connect with to support our progress.

We learn to trust by accepting that we won't always get it right – and that's OK. It's part of the process to distinguish between genuine intuitive impulses and wish-fulfilling everyday desires. Yet if we don't expect our intuition to work, it won't! So initially we may need to *act as if* it's our most trusted guide in decisions relating to our creative expression and authorship – at least until we have some evidence to base our trust upon.

Paying attention to every success, however small, and learning from the instances when we don't hit the mark will quickly build our intuitive capacity. Taking action is part of this process, so dive right in. If something feels right (or wrong), follow through on your feeling and see where it leads. Then pause to reassess before you take your next intuitive steps. Repeat regularly.

Cultivating your intuition will enrich your path as a Conscious Writer at every stage along the way, and in the process you'll discover hidden treasures. The actor Alan Alda puts it like this, 'You have to leave the city of your comfort and go into the wilderness of your intuition. What you'll discover will be wonderful. What you'll discover is yourself.'

# CHAPTER 7

# CONNECTION

Our journey through the seven core principles culminates in connection, which encompasses the full spectrum of qualities that support us in becoming and remaining conscious – as writers and in all areas of our lives.

Connection echoes the non-duality of the first core principle, presence, and we realize that separating these principles is only a way of understanding and engaging with their individual characteristics until they become second nature. Ultimately, we come to embrace the reality that they all reflect one exquisite whole, just like a rainbow refracting the light of the sun. This one whole naturally includes us. As William James expressed it, 'We are like islands in the sea, separate on the surface but connected in the deep.'

Feeling connected is crucial for most people's sense of health and wellbeing. In fact, numerous studies over the last 50 years have shown that a sense of connection is more closely linked to happiness and high self-esteem than wealth, fame and even physical health. Research has shown that social connection strengthens our immune system and leads to a 50 per cent increased chance of longevity. Conversely, those who feel disconnected experience greater health issues like obesity, high blood pressure and depression. In fact, a landmark survey has shown that a lack of social connection 'predicts vulnerability to disease and death above and beyond traditional risk factors such as smoking'.[1]

At a deeper level, the reality is that we don't need to feel connected to anyone or anything in order to experience a true sense of connection that equates with a complete sense of primordial wholeness. Researchers agree that the internal feeling of connection is by far the most important factor, and this echoes the findings of both perennial wisdom and contemporary science.

As Chief Seattle famously expressed, 'This we know: all things are connected like the blood that unites us. We do not weave the web of life, we are merely a strand in it. Whatever we do to the web, we do to ourselves.'

From the perspective of Eastern philosophy, Alan Watts, the author of one of the first bestselling books on Zen Buddhism, *The Way of Zen*, concurred, 'I'll tell you what hermits realize. If you go off into a far, far forest and get very quiet, you'll come to understand that you're connected with everything.'[2]

And Lynne McTaggart, whose work as a bestselling author, researcher and lecturer has been described as 'a bridge between science and spirituality', sums up the view of new science with this succinct yet impactful statement: 'The universe is connected by a vast quantum energy field.' All life is an expression of that in the world of form.

Whatever route we take into the core of connection, we discover that the fundamental nature of the universe and all it contains is inherently one magnificent whole. Yet intellectual understanding can only take us so far. If we want to know the truth for ourselves, we need to have personal experience so that our appreciation arises from the level of true realization. When we realize something fully, we know it from the inside out. We embody the truth of it; it feels alive within the totality of our being rather than sitting exclusively in the penthouse suite of our mind.

This is the essence of the hero's journey that takes us on a quest to know the truth and return to share the fruits of our discoveries. Dr Jude Currivan describes the hero's journey as 'an inner pilgrimage to wholeness', which represents our journey as Conscious Writers into the heart of connection.

## Beyond Separation

How do we cross the threshold and shift beyond the illusion of separation?

Spending time in nature is one of the most powerful and immediate ways to remember what we've always known in our heart of hearts: that we are an expression of the very same life force that gives rise to the Earth in all her natural glory.

Nature is sometimes dramatic and unforgiving, sometimes peaceful and serene. Yet when we immerse ourselves in the natural world and open our hearts to the pulse of life, we are reminded of all that is sacred and feel a primal sense of connection that is unmistakable.

My first visit to a tropical jungle was initially a shock to my system. We'd travelled for what felt like forever on Venezuelan roads riddled with gaping holes and ended up on an undulating dirt track cut through the trees. Finally, we came to the point where the track simply ran out – the proverbial end of the road. As we walked the final stretch to the remote retreat centre, all of my senses were on supreme alert.

Never before had I felt such life all around me, especially at night, when the song of the tree frogs and vibrancy of jungle life escalated to an incredible symphony of sound! The initial feelings of separation from the unfamiliar environment and all it contained soon gave way to an open embrace that felt deeply nurturing. By the time I left, I had a true glimpse of the ease with which native peoples have lived for thousands of years in fruitful harmony and complete connection with nature.

Yet in the 'developed' western world, we have increasingly lost sight of all that is sacred as we have entrenched ourselves in the concrete jungle. Here, separation and isolation have become the norm and contribute demonstrably to the contemporary epidemic of malaise. Studies show that people living in urban environments have a higher prevalence of anxiety disorders and depression, whereas just being out in nature for relatively short periods of time on a regular basis improves the health and vitality of our body, mind and soul.[3]

The heightened sense of wellbeing that comes from connecting with nature includes feelings of awe, vitality, purpose in life, positive emotions and high moment-to-moment awareness – all traits that are associated with a free creative flow.[4] Richard Ryan, professor of psychology at the University of Rochester, states that, 'Nature is fuel for the soul,' and John Keats confirms, 'The poetry of the earth is never dead.'

## Dive in

- Think of a time when you were stopped in your tracks by the wonder of a mind-blowing sunset, sunlight glistening on the waves of the ocean or a richly coloured hummingbird with wings moving faster than the naked eye can see.

- Immerse yourself in the blissful sensations that arise within you as you recall your experience and make a commitment to creating regular opportunities for such awe-inspiring natural moments when your mind is still and you're simply connected with all that is.

- If this feels unfamiliar to you, schedule time in your diary right now to visit your local park, woodland or any area of natural beauty. Go early in the morning or towards the end of the day when it's quiet and open your heart to the pulse of life all around you. Breathe it right through you and, if possible, walk barefoot on the ground, sit on the earth and lean against an ancient tree to feel the sense of connection that comes from letting go and embracing the essence of nature.

- Take a notepad and pen, and once you sense the shift from separation to connection, if it feels appropriate, pour the energy onto the page and see which words reflect your experience back to you.

- Finally, take forwards the importance of immersing yourself in the realization of wholeness and connection on a regular basis. In addition to going out to experience the natural world, bring it in to your home environment. Have fresh flowers on your desk and plants indoors to remind you that feelings of isolation and separation are an illusion. You'll benefit at every level of everyday life, including creative expression in all its forms, when you remember that connection underlies all that is.

## Connection for Conscious Writers

For Conscious Writers, the principle of connection finds expression in two fundamental ways:

### 1. Inner Connection with Our True Self

The most important is conscious connection with our true self, the eternal part of us that is naturally immersed in Oneness.

Conscious Writing is all about the shift from the sense of separation at the level of our everyday self into the sense of connection at the level of our true self and the mystery that lies beyond. As we've already seen, when we express ourselves creatively from this level, the content that pours through us has a timeless quality that reflects the wholeness from which it arises.

Like the shamans of native traditions, as Conscious Writers we learn to walk between worlds, to journey to other realms and to return to share original insights, fresh perspectives and compelling stories to enrich the lives of others.

# Dive in

- The practices and suggestions outlined on our voyage through the seven core principles are all designed to open the way to inner connection with your true self. You simply need to make time and space to engage with them on a regular basis to know yourself at this level beyond any shadow of doubt.

## 2. Outer Connection with Our Readers

### On the Page

Sharing the fruits of our conscious connection with our true self takes shape through the words we write on the page.

Writing is an exceptionally rich and multi-faceted means of communication that has the potential to transform people's lives in a multitude of ways. Conscious Writing elevates this potential to the highest level of art, peeling away the veils of everyday illusion and speaking directly to the divine spark within us all. The greatest works of art cut through our mental chatter with an awe-inspiring vibration of timeless truth that calls forth in us the clear view of awakened perception. Even if it lasts no longer than a moment, the memory of the experience lingers, and without even realizing it, we are changed forever.

As Conscious Writers, our words express our individual choice of content and we connect with our readers through what we say and how we say it – the ultimate expression of our authentic writer's voice.

Our readers need to resonate with the living reality our words are pointing towards in order to feel the full impact of what we're writing about. They also need to resonate with us as the creators of the experience our writing delivers and the feelings generated from reading our work.

To facilitate these processes, we include points of reference in our writing that provide readers with open doors through which they immediately see what we're saying through *their own eyes*. This is how they understand the way in which our words apply to them as individuals, which is an essential element of the reading experience.

These points of reference include many of the components writers have used since the earliest days of the written word. Perhaps the most powerful of these are the stories and examples that show our message in tangible terms that our readers can grasp. The sense of connection comes through recognition of something similar in their personal realm of experience. Whether we're writing a short story, a full-length novel or a memoir where the story is the totality of the work, certain scenes will resonate more with some readers than with others. All good writing includes opportunities for connection to suit a wide variety of people.

## Dive in

- Create your own Conscious Writing 'Storybook' as a digital or physical location to store your stories. Collect examples from everyday life to illustrate the message you want to communicate. These can be from your own experience as well as from that of people you know, especially those with relevance to the topic you're writing about.

- If you're not yet sure what topic you're going to write about, gather a collection of stories you feel inspired by, as and when you come across them. See this as an ongoing part of your Conscious Writing practice so you'll always have new stories and fresh examples ready for inclusion in your latest writing project.

### In the World

Alongside crafting the words to communicate what we're most passionate about sharing, we also have direct interaction with our readers.

Long gone are the ivory towers populated by reclusive authors whose books succeeded despite their absence from the world stage. As authors today, we need to show up and be visible as ambassadors for our message or be content to paddle in the shallow waters of minimal reach for our work.

Whether we are published via the traditional or self-publishing route, having our own audience of interested readers has become a contemporary Holy Grail. The multitude of ways we provide opportunities for our readers to connect with us – through blogging, speaking, social media and more – are the components of our 'author platform'.

As Conscious Writers, we stand tall at the centre of this wheel and invoke the guidance of our true self, which is of course expressed through the vehicle of our everyday self. In this way, we radiate the frequency of our core truth consciously and creatively into the world through what we think, say and do, and even more importantly, through who we are.

The presence we have as authors in the world and the authenticity of our spoken as well as our written voice serve to draw our ideal readers towards our range of offerings. Books may be just one component of our creative communications and readers will always want to have some kind of connection with their favourite authors.

# Dive in

- Don't wait until your book is written to start building your authentic author platform. Take action *now* to learn what you need to know to write a lively blog, create meaningful connections on social media and establish your expertise in your area.

- Research online for courses, classes and teachers who resonate with you personally. Make sure that whoever you choose to work with is 'walking their talk' and already achieving the results you're looking for.

- Above all, make conscious choices and stay true to yourself and the intentions you have for your authorship - you don't have to engage with everything that's on offer!

As Conscious Writers, the more openings we create for our readers to connect with us through our words on the page and our presence as authors in the world, the greater the potential our writing has to deliver our intended results.

# PART II

## Diving into Creative Flow

# Connecting with Your Creative Core

Having met the 'conscious' in Conscious Writing through an exploration of the seven core principles, we now need to carry forwards the awareness we've cultivated and connect with the core creative impulse. As we dive into the depths of creative flow, we create the internal space out of which pour all forms of creative expression.

The idea to paint some dried thistle heads I'd found on one of my forays into the natural world felt electrifying. I was drawn to them by the wonderful shape and structure of the sharp spikes at the top of the long, thin stems. At seven years old, I didn't hesitate in laying out paints and brushes on the low white table I used for my varied projects. I remembered to wear my red apron, and even put a layer of newspaper underneath, just as I'd been taught to do. This was going to be fun!

I chose the largest brush and joyfully began to paint the first thistle head – first one colour, then another, and another. It was tricky to get the paint right inside the spiky head so that all of the thistles were covered in colour, but I found a way with a mixture of different-sized brushes. The stem was easy and quick to do, and soon my first one was complete.

I didn't stop there. Immersed completely in the process and utterly oblivious to anything else, I continued to paint all of the thistle heads in my collection using a multitude of colours in different combinations. Transforming these dramatic brown gifts from nature into the brightly coloured visions of my imagination absorbed me completely. Even the sharp points of the spikes pricking my small fingers didn't deflect the momentum of this creative endeavour.

When I ran out of thistle heads, I ran downstairs, excitedly looking for my mother to show her what I'd created. I led her back to my room, where the fruits of my efforts were displayed. At first she smiled and seemed pleased to see what I'd come up with. Then her gaze was drawn away from my beautiful thistle heads to the walls of my room. Her sharp intake of breath directed my eyes towards what had stopped her in her tracks. A mass of multi-coloured specks of paint now adorned the area around my creative space. My immediate reaction was to see this as an improvement on the plain colour underneath, but I soon realized from the look on my mother's face that she didn't approve.

I'd been so absorbed in my creative process that I hadn't noticed how each brushstroke on each spike had flicked colour onto the walls as well as onto my cherished thistle heads. My heart sank as I realized what had happened and I spent the next few hours helping my mother wash the paint off the walls before it became a permanent feature!

## The In-Breath and the Out-Breath of Conscious and Creative Living

Losing conscious awareness of ourselves and everything beyond our creative focus is typical of flow – in children and adults alike. Conscious Writing, however, invites us to remain fully conscious and present as we dive into the deepest levels of creative flow while simultaneously releasing our identification with our everyday self and our environment. Immersing ourselves in true conscious awareness, we naturally resonate with insight from the unconscious and archetypal realms and the mystery beyond.

As we saw in Part I, the word 'conscious' points towards the process of self-realization that is a journey to the very core of who we are. This is the 'in-breath' of conscious and creative living.

We 'breathe in' by turning our gaze inwards and dissolving the veils of everyday conditioning in the crucible of conscious awareness. Opening our heart and mind to release all that obscures our true nature, we commit to strengthening our capacity to remain consciously connected to this clear view.

From here, the 'out-breath' flows naturally as the creative impulse draws us towards self-expression.

We 'breathe out' by offering the gifts we've received from our glimpse of infinite potential and shaping the essence into forms that resonate with us at the deepest levels.

As Conscious Writers, we manifest the creative 'out-breath' in the words we write and the actions we take as authors in the world. Yet Conscious Creativity as the interplay of self-realization and self-expression can be applied to any and all forms of creative expression, including how we shape the fundamental fabric of our lives.

Ultimately, our trajectory takes us through co-creation to Creation as we write, and live, in an increasingly permanent state of conscious and creative flow.

# CHAPTER 8

# EXPLORING CREATIVITY AS A CONSCIOUS ENQUIRY

Creativity is defined in a multitude of different ways, from the mundane to the metaphysical, with quantum insight capturing the cutting-edge scientific view.

Rollo May points to the conscious component in his book *The Courage to Create* when he explains that, 'Creativity is the process of bringing something new into being. It requires passion and commitment. It brings to our awareness what was previously hidden and points to new life. The experience is one of heightened consciousness: ecstasy.'[1]

In addition to bringing something into being that didn't exist before, creativity also includes reshaping something that already exists into a new form, and combining ideas or materials in an original way.

The word 'paper', for example, is derived from the word *papyrus*, which refers to a plant found in Egypt along the lower Nile river. About 5,000 years ago, Egyptians harvested, peeled and sliced sheets of papyrus into strips that were then layered and smoothed, providing a flat surface on which to write.

Three thousand years later, a more refined grade of paper came out of China. An innovator called Ts'ai Lun took the fibres of bamboo and the inner bark of a mulberry tree, mixed them with water and pounded them with a wooden tool. After pouring the mixture through a woven cloth and allowing it to dry, he found the fibres created a quality writing surface. Knowledge of this new creation quickly spread throughout China and led to paper becoming one of the most significant creative inventions in history.

Yet creativity isn't restricted to activities that are usually defined as creative, such as making new discoveries or creating the numerous forms that make up the magnificent spectrum of artistic expression. Essentially, it involves seeing the world with fresh eyes and expressing ourselves imaginatively in *all* areas of life, including how we cook our food, choose our clothes and apply ourselves to our work. With a creative mindset, we can make anything a creative act.

## Nine Dots to New Horizons

The bright light that creativity shines in the world has attracted attention from those who have been drawn to understand and enhance the creative impulse we all have. Over the last 50 years, a huge number of tests have been developed to assess the qualities and abilities that constitute creative aptitude. One of these is especially significant in relation to the conscious approach we are interested in as Conscious Writers.

The nine dots puzzle originally appeared in Sam Loyd's 1914 *Cyclopedia of Puzzles* and was adopted by management consultants in the 1970s and 1980s who were intent on encouraging their clients to 'think outside the box'.[2] This now clichéd phrase has been widely used to refer to expanding the boundaries of conventional thinking and clearing the way for more unconventional perspectives to arise. It's also a clue to the solution for the nine dots puzzle.

Here's how it works: the challenge is to connect each of the nine dots using just four continuous straight lines without lifting the pen off the paper. If you've not done this before, try it now before looking ahead to find the solution (*see page 84*):

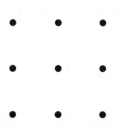

*Figure 2: The Nine Dots Challenge*

When you've confirmed the answer, you'll see that the significance for us as Conscious Writers is the clear message that connecting to our creative core requires us to cross the invisible threshold that separates the comfort of what we know from the uncertainty of what we don't. Having the courage to break out of the box, let go of certainties and face the mystery fearlessly leads us directly into the uncharted waters of infinite creative potential. As French author André Gide puts it, 'One does not discover new lands without consenting to lose sight of the shore.'

## Into the Mystery

Yet entering the mystery and embracing 'not knowing' at the level of the mind provides many of us with a real challenge. We've largely been taught to prize knowledge and avoid ignorance by applying ourselves diligently to learning.

We usually don't admit to not knowing something in order to avoid the shame that is often associated with ignorance. Instead, we bluff our way through or rapidly do some research to discover what it is we think we ought to know.

In fact it's the feeling that we *should* know when we don't that results in such distress. This is especially significant in relation to creativity, as it causes a contraction to occur at the subtle levels within us that effectively blocks the creative flow. The word 'should' is always a sign that the conditioned reactions of the everyday self are at work!

### Zoë's Story

*Zoë knew she was stuck with her writing but didn't know what to do about it. She felt that she should know how to write her book because she'd been teaching the content for a long time. However, she was struggling with communicating the depth of her work on the page. Her anxiety was escalating and she was on the brink of giving up.*

*Then a friend suggested she contact me. In the course of our in-depth session, it surfaced that Zoë was terrified of what she thought of as 'the emptiness' of not knowing. She saw it as a 'dark space' to be avoided, since each time she looked towards it she experienced a distinct sense of discomfort.*

*When I explained that her fear of not knowing was the underlying cause of her creative block and the empty space was in fact full of creative potential, she began to see the situation differently. This was a real turning-point for her at every level.*

*With guidance and support, Zoë was able to face the emptiness without fear and soon discovered that embracing the feeling of not knowing actually opened up space for a much deeper level of Knowing to arise.*

*It took a while for her to live the reality of this discovery on a day-to-day basis. Yet she stayed with all she'd learned during the course of our work together and did uncover the depth she was looking for in relation to writing her book. What she hadn't anticipated was how much she'd discover about herself along the way.*

Exploring creativity as a conscious enquiry involves making many new discoveries in the unknown realms of the mystery and beyond. As author Jyrki Vainonen advises, we have to 'Dive again and again into the river of uncertainty. Create in the dark, only then can you recognize the light.'

As Conscious Writers, we learn to identify the uncertainty as a product of the everyday self and accept it fully as an integral part of the creative process. This allows a deeper level of Knowing to arise from our true self and enables us to accept the invitation that Conscious Writing offers us: to engage consciously with the mystery and become a co-creator with it.

## Dive in

- One of the questions I asked Zoë to play with as part of this process was 'What if...?'

- Think of a creative challenge you're currently facing and ask yourself, 'What if it didn't matter that I don't know what to do?'

- Write freely using 'What if?' to guide your stream of consciousness towards completely accepting not knowing.

- Once you experience a sense of openness towards not knowing, ask yourself, 'What if I did know? How might it look, sound, feel?'

- Allow your writing to arise from the open space of fully accepting the not knowing and simply explore possibilities on the page. Sooner or later, clarity will come.

## Living the Questions

The opening that's created through genuine acceptance of not knowing also enables us to take the next step on our journey: to 'live the questions' until the answers present themselves. In his timeless book *Letters to a Young Poet*, Rainer Maria Rilke advised his young protégé to: 'Have patience with everything unresolved in your heart and try to love the questions themselves as if they were locked rooms or books written in a foreign language. The point is to live everything. Live the questions now. Perhaps then, someday far in the future, you will gradually, without even noticing it, live your way into the answers.'[3]

Adopting a conscious approach to creativity facilitates living the questions in a way that usually delivers the answers in a shorter time-frame than Rilke implies. Remaining open to all possibilities as we follow the golden thread of our creative impulses leads us to discover, rather than presuppose, the final form our ideas are destined to take. This is how we unlock 'the rooms', learn the 'foreign language' the books are written in and eventually uncover the treasures they contain.

Living the questions lies at the core of our exploration into the heart of creativity and leads to the realization that creativity is essentially a profound process of open enquiry. David Ulrich, author of the inspiring book on the seven stages of creativity *The Widening Stream*, confirms that:

> 'Creativity must remain an inquiry; it defies logic and arises from a deeper region than the ordinary mind's domain ...

*It is only through a wide and deep engagement with the process, undertaken with a sense of "not knowing", that we may begin to understand it.'[4]*

## How Do We Do That?

Living the questions of our individual creative endeavours as Conscious Writers requires us to draw on all that we've learned in Part I about becoming and remaining conscious and to prioritize being fully present to the unfolding process.

But once we've clarified the direction of our creative focus, we simply let go. Specifically, we release the effort related to the intellectual habit of grasping for answers. The more we're able to let the questions be while we engage in supportive conscious actions, the faster the answers are likely to pour through the open invitation our surrender creates.

Sometimes the answers arrive as individual pieces of a jigsaw that gradually make up the creative picture we're working on. On other occasions, the whole vision arrives in an instant and we then spend time clothing the essence in forms that are congruent with the living truth the vision reflects.

## Dive in

Here are some suggestions for conscious actions that emphasize *being* rather than *doing* to support you with living your creative questions.

Begin by identifying your creative intention, such as seeking clarity on how to organize your ideas for the next chapter of your book or a blog post you want to write on a particular topic.

Then give yourself permission to make time and space for the following conscious actions.

Avoid intellectual analysis and allow whatever arises in your awareness to take shape gradually.

When ideas relating to your question arrive, write them down in note form without losing the spaciousness of your experience.

Finally, when you feel ready, gather up your notes and use them as the basis for living your way fully into the answers you're seeking.

- *Reflection and Contemplation:* Gaze softly at passing clouds or into a reflective surface like the still water of a pond, as I did by the wildlife pond (*on page xi*). Immerse yourself in present-moment awareness and enjoy an alert yet relaxed and spacious experience of being.

- *Silence and Solitude:* Maintain the energetic integrity of your conscious enquiry by spending time alone with your question(s) and prioritizing inner and outer silence. Avoid distractions of all kinds by turning off notifications on your phone and removing yourself from real or virtual contact with other people for the duration of this practice.

- *Listen to Music:* In addition to immersing yourself in silence and solitude, on another occasion you may choose to listen to music that opens your heart and inspires your soul. Although scientific opinions vary regarding the contribution music makes to intelligence and creativity, if it works for you, use it!

- *Take Your Questions for a Walk:* Walking has been a favoured pastime of many well-known writers, including William Wordsworth, James Joyce and Virginia Woolf. The physical activity and rhythm of walking help to trigger new ideas and patterns of thought, especially when you're fully present to the process of walking.

- *Dream Incubation:* The surrealist painter Salvador Dali used to draw on ideas triggered by the hypnagogic state, which occurs between waking and sleeping, and dreams have been used for thousands of years for spiritual and creative insight. Learning to have lucid dreams – dreams in which you're aware you're dreaming – can provide endless opportunities for resolving creative questions.

As an immediate dream incubation technique, try this:

Last thing at night, write the focus of your enquiry down on a piece of paper and set a clear intention to receive an answer from your dreams. Engage your mind and emotions to create a positive belief that you *will* receive an answer of some kind and that you *will* remember your dreams.

Put the paper under your pillow, and a pen and some paper by your bed, and fall asleep with your intention clear in your mind and heart.

As soon as you wake, before moving your body, recall your dreams in as much detail as you can remember. Make some notes straight away and write up the detail later. Review the dream for symbolic clues that provide insight into the questions(s) you've asked.

If nothing comes to you during or after these practices, just accept that as your reality at this time. Avoid feeling disappointed or impatient. Simply continue with the other components of your everyday life and return to one or more of the options another time.

The best rhythm to adopt over a period of days, weeks or more, depending on the scale of your question(s), is to intersperse these conscious actions with your regular commitments. Continue diving in, surfacing and refocusing until you feel you have what you need to take your next steps.

Learning to live the questions is an integral part of the creative process for Conscious Writers and leads to three additional keys that unlock the door to a life of rich and rewarding conscious and creative expression.

# Three Creative Keys

## 1. Trust

The open heart/open mind approach we've been discussing leads directly to deepening our capacity to trust.

All creative projects require a degree of trust if new discoveries are to be made. We can place our trust in the creative process, our true self, the universe or a combination of these and other conduits of grace to suit our individual preference.

Trust is developed and strengthened by repeatedly stepping off metaphorical cliffs and finding that we *do* have the wings required to fly. Sooner or later we realize that trust opens the way for us to fulfil our true creative potential and create what we're here to create.

## 2. Commitment

The following words by William H. Murray express the significance of commitment beautifully:

*'Until one is committed, there is hesitancy, the chance to draw back. Concerning all acts of initiative (and creation), there is one elementary truth, the ignorance of which kills countless ideas and splendid plans: that the moment one definitely commits oneself, then Providence moves too. All sorts of things occur to help one that would never otherwise have occurred. A whole stream of events issues from the decision, raising in one's favour all manner of unforeseen incidents and meetings and material assistance, which no man could have dreamed would have come his way. Whatever you can do, or dream you can do, begin it. Boldness has genius, power, and magic in it. Begin it now.'[5]*

Taking one step at a time, we combine trust with genuine commitment to begin our creative work and then show up, and continue showing up come what may until we've finished. Commitment raises the bar on making time and space to work on our creative projects from optional to mandatory.

## 3. Surrender

At the level of the everyday self, we think we're responsible for making everything happen. At the level of our true self, we know we're part of one magnificent whole and have access to an abundant stream of insight and guidance when we surrender the will of the everyday self to greater awareness.

As we cross the threshold of conscious and active surrender, we let go of perfection once and for all and focus on the transformative nature of the unfolding process as an end in its own right. This is how we are truly empowered to release our attachment to the end results of our creative actions and in doing so allow the outcome to be what it will be. Usually, this will far surpass our original expectations.

Verses 8–9 of the *Tao Te Ching* provide us with the following counsel: 'Do your work, then step back. The only path to serenity.'

## Quantum Creativity

Physicist Amit Goswami, PhD, provides us with a quantum bridge between ancient wisdom and advanced science that reveals a new scientific basis for the conscious approach to creativity we're exploring.

Dr Goswami was a full professor in the Department of Physics at the University of Oregon, where he served from 1968 to 1997. He is a pioneer of the new paradigm of science called 'science within consciousness', an idea he explicated in his seminal book *The Self-Aware Universe*, where he also solved the quantum measurement problem elucidating the famous observer effect. His revolutionary work is based on establishing the primacy of consciousness as the successor to the outdated and fundamentally incomplete primacy of matter around which our everyday world is largely constructed.

In his ground-breaking book *Quantum Creativity*, he explains that according to quantum physics, there are two levels of reality: possibility and actuality. This leads to what he calls 'quantum thinking', which draws on the conscious mind of actuality and the unconscious mind of possibility. He elaborates, 'Manifest matter is preceded by quantum possibilities or potentialities.' Creativity involves 'conscious choice [which] collapses the possibilities into manifest actuality... Since this choice is made from a state of consciousness beyond the ego [derived from a conditioned simple hierarchy of learned programmes], we refer to it as 'higher' or 'quantum' consciousness; spiritual traditions refer to it as God.'

We experience quantum consciousness through our quantum self, which in Conscious Writing we call our true self, and this co-creates with the ego or everyday self. The creative 'freedom and spontaneity' of the quantum self 'overrules deliberation and past conditioning' and the ego 'contributes its expertise, its learned repertoire of past context with which to make representations of the new'. This is how the everyday self acts as the vehicle of expression for our true self in all forms of creative expression.

In addition, Dr Goswami identifies two categories of creativity: 'Outer creativity relates to problem-solving in the arts and sciences and inner creativity ... involves the discovery of deeper truth and the realm of spiritual growth... Both inner and outer creativity are about freedom ...

outer creativity should become the expression of your inner freedom in the outer world.'

Conscious Writing invites us to combine inner and outer creativity and express our inner freedom through the words we write and the actions we take as authors in the world.

Finally, from the perspective of the big picture, Dr Goswami also confirms that, 'We become most creative in our lives when we recognize that the cosmos is trying to act through us… Evolution is fundamentally creative, and when we align ourselves with the evolutionary movements of consciousness, the universe itself puts wind in our sails.'[6]

## Conscious Creativity

As we complete our exploration of creativity as a conscious enquiry, it is obvious from both scientific and spiritual perspectives that creativity is so much more than just something we do. It is a state of being that adds colour, depth and richness to everyday life.

Conscious Creativity is fundamentally an expression of who we are and a path to the heart of freedom, where we discover that we are the microcosm in the creative impulse of life itself. Artists since the dawn of time have been inspired to express the awe and wonder of such profound realizations that bypass the mind and speak directly through the heart and soul.

Conscious Creativity leads to profound inner transformation *and* original outer expression in whatever forms we engage with. This is because first and foremost we prioritize being fully conscious and commit ourselves to Truth in a way that resonates with our individual characteristics. Our presence then invites the dance of focus and flow to include us in its rhythm and we spontaneously become the instrument for the music to play through our thoughts, words and actions.

Ultimately, we become aligned with the process of Creation and express the Truth consciously and creatively in each and every moment of our lives.

⌣

## The Nine Dots Solution

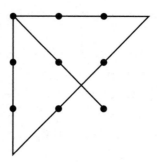

*Figure 3: The Nine Dots Solution*

The resolution to the nine dots challenge (*see page 74*) comes from seeing beyond the box that the mind automatically assumes exists when presented with the nine dots image. Mentally breaking free of the non-existent boundary leads to the answer.

# CHAPTER 9

# CULTIVATING YOUR RELATIONSHIP WITH CREATIVITY

The exploration of creativity as a conscious enquiry has directed our gaze towards creativity as a way of being as well as referring to specific actions we take to craft something new. Now it's time to investigate our individual relationship to it.

## How Schools Kill Creativity

Astonishingly, we are rarely taught how to cultivate our natural creativity as part of the skill set required for adult life. In fact the opposite is usually the case. Children are naturally creative, yet the western education system strongly emphasizes the importance of learning facts and figures alongside developing a finely tuned intellect for the purposes of problem-solving and analytical thought. Useful though these skills may be, when they are gained in isolation we are effectively being taught – directly and indirectly – to grow out of creativity. As a result, many of us leave school valuing our rational mind to the exclusion of creativity, which becomes reserved for the gifted few.

In 2006, creativity expert Sir Ken Robinson gave an inspiring and entertaining talk for an official TED conference called *How Schools Kill Creativity*. In just under 20 minutes, he made a strong case for creating an education system that nurtures, rather than undermines, creativity. The presentation struck a chord with a massive global audience and continues to do so today. At the time of writing, it has been watched 31,233,036 times. In it, Robinson states that creativity, which he defines as 'the process of having original ideas that have value', is as important as literacy, yet our education system has placed the arts at the bottom of the educational hierarchy.[1] Clearly something has gone awry.

When this kind of education is combined with pressures from family and society to comply with perceived ideals of achievement and success, a high proportion of us understandably feel disconnected from the natural creative impulse we all have. It becomes buried under logic and learning and we're left struggling to value it sufficiently to make it a priority in our lives.

As Conscious Writers, even when we manage to admit an inclination to express ourselves creatively on the page, it remains a serious challenge to legitimize making the time and space required. In fact, one of the greatest challenges of aspiring authors is finding enough hours in the day to write. Upon investigation, however, it becomes clear that other, more 'serious' commitments are usually taking precedence over writing and the creative nurturing it needs. Ultimately, we'll never *find* the time for creativity and writing; we have to *make* the time by consciously setting our priorities and *claiming* that space in our schedules as sacred.

The first step for many of us is to reconnect fully with our natural creativity so we can find our way to the page and write freely from the level of our true self. An important part of this process involves letting go of the learned patterns of limiting belief and behaviour that have been so effectively 'schooled' into us at the level of the everyday self. These are the ties that hold us back from realizing our true creative potential.

## Jack's Story

*Jack was brought up with extremely negative associations relating to creativity and the word games he enjoyed so much as a child. As he grew older, he was increasingly overruled when he showed interest in creative pursuits and not allowed to choose how to spend his time, either at home or at school. Instead he was required to focus on passing his exams in order to 'have a good career'.*

As a young man, Jack slowly began to edge away from his early conditioning and move towards work that included some of the creative components his soul longed for. After short stints in serious roles, eventually he found himself working as a copywriter, at which he excelled. However, he viewed it simply as work he had to do in order to move on to greater achievements so he could succeed in the eyes of others. He was completely blocked from receiving any praise for his skills because a part of him was living out the reality he'd been taught. Yet deep inside he felt a constant 'knocking' on an inner door. Before long, he couldn't ignore it.

Reaching out for help was a huge step, and once he'd crossed that threshold, his watershed moment came quickly. For the first time he was able to take a step back and see how his love of creativity had been 'trashed' as he was growing up. With support, he was able to begin the process of releasing his negative beliefs around creativity and setting himself free to make choices for himself about what to include in his life.

As his awareness grew, he started to accept that his copywriting skills did have value. Perhaps even more importantly, they became the foundation for him to reconnect with his childhood love of poetry. He started writing his own poems and in time found the courage to connect with other poets, who further validated his progress.

It wasn't long before Jack was invited to submit some poems for publication in a collection and soon after he began performing some of his poetry at local events. He surprised himself by loving the performances as much as the writing!

As his mindset continued to shift and his confidence in his natural creative ability developed, he felt ready to change his work situation to incorporate his new-found creative freedom into his 'day job'.

Jack is continuing to build his creative muscles as he reshapes his life to reflect his inner truth.

Jack's upbringing may sound harsh in relation to creativity, but we all have limiting beliefs which frequently demean our capacity to create and our ability to write. Knowing that these are a product of our everyday self, we need to start where we currently are and appreciate the true power our beliefs have over us.

## The Power of Belief

Beliefs are essentially ideas, assumptions, views and opinions we've accumulated over time about ourselves and the world. They are lodged at such a deep level within us that we accept them as true and base our lives around them, even when evidence exists that they are false.

In a recent article called 'The Two Kinds of Belief', Alex Lickerman, MD, explains that there is a growing recognition in neuropsychology of just how irrational our rational thinking can be:

> 'We now know that our intellectual value judgments –
> that is, the degree to which we believe or disbelieve an
> idea – are powerfully influenced by our brains' proclivity
> for attachment. Our brains are attachment machines,
> attaching not just to people and places, but to ideas.
> And not just in a coldly rational manner. Our brains
> become intimately emotionally entangled with ideas
> we come to believe are true (however we came to that
> conclusion) and emotionally allergic to ideas we believe
> to be false. This emotional dimension to our rational
> judgment explains a gamut of measurable biases that
> show just how unlike computers our minds are.'[2]

We all have many kinds of bias; Lickerman goes on to clarify two of them:

1. *Confirmation bias:* This causes us to notice and select evidence that supports what we already believe to be true and completely ignore anything that contradicts our existing beliefs.

2.  *Disconfirmation bias:* This causes us to work hard at actually disproving evidence that disagrees with any aspect of the belief system we have invested time and emotion in developing as our own.

Essentially, we continually verify what we already believe and deny evidence to the contrary. So, if we don't believe creativity is valid or think that we lack creative ability, we'll repeatedly prove ourselves right.

Mahatma Gandhi put it like this: 'If I believe I cannot do something, it makes me incapable of doing it. But when I believe I can, then I acquire the ability to do it even if I didn't have it in the beginning.'

## Conscious vs Unconscious

In order to grasp fully the immense power our beliefs have over us, we need to appreciate the substantial role our unconscious mind plays in how we perceive, act and react to the world around us.

The unconscious includes all of the thoughts, feelings, memories, associations, habits and implicit knowledge (what we have learned so well that we do it without conscious thought, like driving) from our experience of life. It's like a library that contains everything, including our beliefs, and is constantly processing massive amounts of sensory data so that our conscious mind can focus exclusively on immediate priorities.

The unconscious mind attracts our conscious attention through emotion. Feeling anxious, for example, may be a sign of potential physical danger or it may indicate a more subtle level of threat, which could be to the stability of our belief system. The unconscious also learns quickly, makes associations and works to protect us from harm. If we were shamed for a poorly written essay at school, our unconscious may try to guard against such ridicule in the future. One way to achieve this would be to cause us to feel anxious about writing something that will be judged by others. This may effectively block us from wanting to write anything other than shopping lists.

When we are young, our unconscious mind is totally open to suggestion. As a result, assumptions and beliefs both positive and negative find fertile ground and with any degree of repetition grow into strong patterns that affect us unconsciously for our whole lives.

As adults, most of us believe we're capable of making conscious choices. Whether we're deciding what to wear or how to earn our living, we think we're in charge of making clear decisions about what will suit us best. However, this is simply not the case. An abundance of research shows that we're usually deluding ourselves about the conscious nature of our choices. Instead, we're routinely fired by unconscious patterns that were created in our most formative years and beliefs about what we should or shouldn't be doing with our time.

This is why we can set an intention to make time and space for writing yet repeatedly fail to make it a reality. The unconscious mind is far more powerful than the everyday conscious mind and it may have a shadow intention that overrules the intention we think we've set.

The more we fail to follow through with our creative intentions, the more we confirm our beliefs about how incapable we obviously are. And so the cycle repeats … until we shine the light of *true* awareness from the level of our true self onto the loop we're caught in and *then* take conscious action to set ourselves free.

The way we do this is to apply what we've learned about becoming conscious and then identify the beliefs, both positive and negative, that we have around creativity so we can develop the former and liberate ourselves from the latter.

## The Five-Step Process

Beliefs aren't just thoughts in the mind; they usually have powerful emotions attached. They are like energy frozen in the body right down to the cellular level. Releasing some deeply rooted beliefs requires professional help. Fortunately, there are many options available today, such as the powerful energy-healing technique of Life Alignment, which Philippa Lubbock eloquently explains in her comprehensive book of the same name.[3]

However, we can make genuine progress with shifting our belief structure ourselves as long as we approach the task with as much true-self awareness as we are able to bring to it.

The following five-step process is for discovering the beliefs you currently have in relation to creativity and letting go of those that aren't serving you. Allow plenty of time on your own and without interruption so you feel spacious enough for deep exploration and release. Take breaks between the steps if necessary to process your thoughts and feelings – walking in nature is always a good option – and rest when you need to.

This process can also be applied to other areas of your life, including writing. Simply adapt the questions in Step 1 accordingly.

## Dive in

### Step 1: Record

Begin by using any of the techniques from Part I to bring yourself into a present and aligned state in which you are open to insight arising from your true self. Then reflect on and answer the following questions in your Conscious Writing Journal:

- When you were a child, what did you most enjoy doing in your free time? If you weren't allowed to do what you wanted, how would you have liked to spend your time?

- What were you actively encouraged to be and do?

- What were you actively discouraged from being and doing?

- What attitude did your parents and teachers have towards creativity?

- In what ways did you experience and express yourself creatively when you were growing up?

- Have you continued to express yourself creatively as an adult? If so, in what ways? If not, why do you think that is the case?

- What does creativity mean to you now?

- Do you think of yourself as a creative person?

- Do you believe that you have creative potential that has yet to be developed?

- How important do you believe creativity is to your happiness and wellbeing?

### Step 2: Summarize

Review your answers and…

- Start a fresh page in your journal, take a blank sheet of paper or type up a digital summary of the *positive supporting beliefs* you've identified from the questions above. Date your work and keep it safely. When you look back in years to come, you may be surprised at how much your beliefs have changed, especially relating to the last few questions.

- Now take another blank piece of paper and this time write by hand the *negative limiting beliefs* that have surfaced from your investigation. Do some stream-of-consciousness writing about each one to add to your initial answers so that by the time you've finished you feel completely empty of thoughts and feelings relating to each belief.

### Step 3: Release

Give yourself full permission to release your limiting beliefs and act as if you have the ability to do it instantly. Commit yourself to that reality and now:

- Reread what you've written about your limiting beliefs.

- Set the clearest intention you're able to create at this time and put your will into dissolving and releasing the restrictive beliefs from your body, emotions and mind.

- Smile and acknowledge the purpose the beliefs may have served until now.

- Feel where these beliefs are in your body and breathe deeply into those areas.

- As you breathe out, affirm your intention to release each belief and imagine it leaving your body like a cloud of dark smoke, which easily disperses and becomes clearer and brighter with each exhale. As you do so…

### Step 4: Tear

- Rip the paper on which you've written your negative beliefs into tiny pieces with as much clarity of intention as you're able to muster. Continue releasing the limiting energy from your body with each exhale until you feel you've finished.

## Step 5: Dispatch

- Collect up the shreds of paper and responsibly burn them or bury them in the ground while respectfully requesting that the earth composts the negative energy these beliefs have held and transforms it back into a neutral state for alternative future use.

This process may seem overly simplistic as a way of ridding ourselves of beliefs that may have blocked us creatively for years. However, complexity and efficacy aren't necessarily correlated. A recent study indicated that writing our negative thoughts down and physically throwing the paper away supports us in discarding those thoughts once and for all.[4] As we've just discovered, our beliefs truly affect the results we experience in life, so be prepared to 'act as if' until personal experience provides verified evidence.

When we engage in this kind of process, we're drawing on the colossal capacity of our brains to be rewired. Neuroscientists used to believe that our brain structure was largely fixed after early childhood. Yet decades of research have revealed that 'experience can actually change both the brain's physical structure (anatomy) and functional organization (physiology)' and the term 'neuroplasticity' refers to 'changes in neural pathways resulting from changes in behaviour, environment, neural processes, thinking, emotions, and changes resulting from bodily injury'.[5]

In short, as we touched on in Chapter 1 in relation to mindfulness training, we can rewire our brain like reprogramming a computer to switch from one set of functional criteria to another. First we release our attachment to the limiting beliefs that hold us back and then we create new mental and emotional connections that support us in realizing our full creative potential.

# Your Creative Vision

Now it's time for you to inject fresh energy into the space that's been created and begin the process of developing new neural pathways to support your creativity and honour your impulse to write.

# Dive in

- Set aside at least an hour and make whatever arrangements are necessary to be alone and without interruption or distraction. You'll need a blank sheet of paper and a pen; you're going to do a mind map.

- Begin with at least five minutes of deep breathing. Relax, close your eyes, turn your attention inwards and let go of the everyday world by focusing on the anchor of your breath.

- When you feel ready, turn the paper sideways, write 'Creativity' in the middle and put the date on the back.

- Brainstorm what creativity means to you now and what role you'd like it to have as your life unfolds in the future. Immerse yourself in a vision that inspires you at every level.

- Write key words from this non-judgemental imaginative process as branches extending out from the centre and allow extensions of your ideas to become sub-branches.

- Feel free to include affirmations such as 'I am a creative person'. These beliefs can be game-changers when you truly inhabit them.

- Explore all areas of life – home, work, relationships – and specific areas of creative activity such as writing where the sub-branches may include a blog, articles for print magazines, short stories, non-fiction, fiction, memoirs and more (*see the example in Figure 4*).

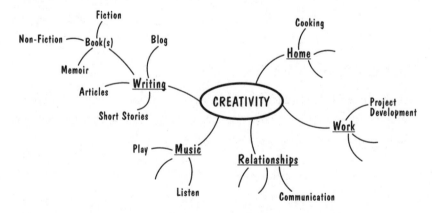

*Figure 4: A Sample Mind Map for Your Creative Vision*

- If you have a sense of timing, be specific and record your intention to start writing now, next month or next year.

- Allow your ideas to flow onto the page without censorship, even if you have no idea *how* these possibilities may become actualities. Stay with the visionary focus and enjoy playing with potential. Add everything to your mind map until it feels complete and you're satisfied that it includes all the components of your creative vision – for now.

- When the process draws to a natural conclusion, put your mind map away and go for a walk or do any kind of conscious movement that appeals to you. Keep a notebook and pen nearby and remain alert for additional inspiration that may come to you over the next few days.

Finally, remember that you have full permission to include whatever forms of creative expression fill your heart and soul with delight. In the words of mystical poet Rumi, 'Let the beauty we love be what we do. There are hundreds of ways to kneel and kiss the ground.'

# CHAPTER 10

# CONNECTING WITH THE WHOLE CREATIVE CYCLE

The big picture of our current creative vision provides us with an overview of the areas that feel significant to us right now, so we work with those and understand they may change and develop over time. From here we begin the process of manifesting our vision, and as Conscious Writers, this involves focusing on our creative writing intentions and all we need to make them a reality.

Before we pick up our pens to write, there is one more aspect we need to address in the process of diving in deeply to creative flow and cultivating the internal space out of which our writing will pour.

## Nurturing Our Creative Soul

Nurturing our creative soul involves frequently filling our inner creative well so that it never runs dry and always allows our creativity to flow freely. Conscious Creativity teaches us to do this by connecting with the whole creative cycle and honouring each and every phase.

Yet such an approach is rarely accepted as a valid use of our precious time. Instead we are drawn by the demands of contemporary life in the western world to busy ourselves with endless 'doing' and direct our energy exclusively outwards to support family and friends, earn our living and maintain our personal space.

While we all need to honour our commitments respectfully, let's remember this process begins with honouring our commitments to ourselves. In the fast lane of doing all that *seems* essential, we often forget to replenish our inner resources beyond basic recharging that sees us through to the next stint on the treadmill of activity. As a result, our output frequently far outweighs the input, so we end up feeling exhausted, empty and eventually resentful and unwell. No wonder creative dreams are so often unfulfilled!

Engaging in any kind of creative project like writing a book entails having the strength and stamina to say the course. Authorship is a big commitment and calls for us to be ready with fresh ideas and creative insights over relatively prolonged periods of time.

It's true that writing and publishing books can be done at an impressively fast rate these days. However, the more usual story is that it takes many months, often years, to write and publish quality books that will stand the test of time. Creativity is involved at every stage, including the birth of the book in the world and ensuring it ends up in the hands of interested readers. Authors need to maintain the momentum of spreading the word well beyond the initial launch if the book is to become fully established instead of sinking without trace.

Conscious Writing respects the duration of this journey and underlines the importance of *how* we get to our intended destination. From a holistic perspective, it isn't enough to arrive regardless of the potential cost to ourselves and our creative outcome. Consequently, as Conscious Writers we prioritize nurturing our creative soul right from the start and continue this practice along the way so our inner well remains topped up and available to provide for whatever creative output is required.

This approach echoes the understanding that conscious and creative living includes phases of 'breathing in' and 'breathing out'. Here, the 'in-breath' signifies filling our creative well and receiving the inspiration to do our work; the 'out-breath' represents giving the fruits of the transformed essence away freely as we express ourselves creatively on the page and in the world.

Nurturing our creative soul is also fundamental to developing and strengthening the new neural pathways we are creating in our brain to support all aspects of our creative expression.

## The Four Phases of the Creative Cycle

Nature offers us a perfect example of the creative cycle. The seasons unfold through the year and reflect back to us the very flow of life itself. The stillness of winter becomes the backdrop to the first shoots appearing in spring as the light and warmth of the sun create the right conditions for the natural world to awaken. The fullness of summer leads eventually to the harvest of autumn before the inevitable return to the sleeping winter state in advance of the cycle beginning again the following year. These natural phases are all exquisitely related and flow effortlessly from one to the other in the cycle of life, death and rebirth.

In creative terms, we've already touched on the value of stillness, silence and space as powerful gateways to presence and the deep authentic part of ourselves that is naturally creative. So it comes as no surprise that the true creative impulse originates here, just like the perennial seeds that require the harsh conditions of winter to germinate.

Our most original creative insights arise from the still depths that lie beyond the intellectual workings of the everyday self. This occurs whether or not we are consciously aware of it and naturally signifies the starting-point for the creative cycle.

The first spark of the creative fire to arrive in our conscious awareness is the initial flash of inspiration, which reflects the early flowers of spring emerging from the bare winter soil. When we feel inspired and in touch with our muse, we effortlessly transcend our everyday self and sense unlimited potential.

As the smouldering blaze burns ever more brightly, our imagination is activated. Ideas are developed and details are added to bring the colours, shapes and textures of our inspiration into full bloom like a magnificent array of summer flowers.

As the wheel turns, our creative harvest becomes visible as our words meet the page and the autumn fruits show up in linguistic form. Here we continue to play with essence and form, back and forth, dipping in and out of earlier phases of inspiration and imagination in a creative dance until we sense the deepest resonance – the moment when our writing fits seamlessly with its subject as if it is one facet of a fractal whole. Then we stop, return to stillness and breathe in deeply before the cycle begins again.

*Figure 5: The Four Phases of the Creative Cycle*

Giving ourselves permission to slow down enough to connect fully with each phase of the creative cycle is one of many significant thresholds we need to cross on our way to becoming fully fledged Conscious Writers. In the process, we learn to live the reality that Gandhi summed up so well: 'There is more to life than simply increasing its speed.'

## Phase 1: Stillness, Silence, Space and Solitude

Stillness, silence and space open the way for us to be present in the moment and bring conscious awareness to our creative expression. Timeless teachings underline the value of these primary conditions for the creative cycle.

Stillness, according to Lao Tzu, leads us to 'become one with heaven and earth' and 'only thus can one manifest the true nature and law of things from within'. This is an elegant description of Conscious Creativity that applies beautifully to our work as Conscious Writers. He continues, 'To the mind that is still, the whole universe surrenders.' From here, we create what we're here to create and write what we're here to write.

Silence has always been an integral part of the contemplative traditions. Monks, nuns, sages and mystics all spend long periods in silence in order to celebrate the Divine. However, we don't have to shut ourselves away to benefit from periods of conscious silence. Even short periods of silence can revolutionize our sense of meaning, purpose and clarity in relation to our creative work and our life in general. Mother Teresa confirms that, 'God cannot be found in noise and restlessness. God is the friend of silence. See how nature – trees, flowers, grass – grows in silence; see the stars, the moon and the sun, how they move in silence... We need silence to be able to touch souls.'

Space is required for us to access our authentic truth and feeds directly into creativity. As author Robert Grudin suggests, 'The creative process might be simplified if we stopped searching for ideas and simply made room for them to visit.' His words also remind us of the inherently feminine nature of this phase of the creative cycle. We 'breathe in' to receive ideas that require space to surface in our conscious awareness.

Finally, solitude is central to awakening consciousness and cultivating creativity. It enables us to focus on our personal connection to universal truth without distraction. When solitude is combined with stillness, silence and space, we learn to hear the whispers of our soul, open our hearts to all of Creation and align ourselves with that.

Wolfgang Amadeus Mozart has given us a delightful insight into his creative process which echoes our exploration and acknowledges solitude:

> 'When I am completely myself, entirely alone and of good cheer – say travelling in a carriage or walking after a good meal or during the night when I cannot sleep; it is on such occasions that my ideas flow best and most abundantly. Whence and how they come I know not; nor can I force them. Those ideas that please me I retain in memory, and if I continue in this way, it soon occurs to me how I may turn this or that morsel to account. All this fires my soul, and provided I am not disturbed, my subject enlarges itself, becomes methodized and defined, and the whole thing, though it may be long, stands almost complete and finished in my mind so that I can survey it like a fine picture or a beautiful statue. What a delight this is I cannot tell! All this inventing, this producing takes place in a pleasing lively dream.'

## Dive in

- Schedule time in your diary now to spend some quality time in solitude and immerse yourself in stillness, silence and space. Make this a regular part of your practice as a Conscious Writer. If being alone is unfamiliar to you, start with short amounts of time and accustom yourself gradually to spending longer periods in creative seclusion. Pay attention to the effect this has on the quality and depth of your creative insight and always begin your writing with a few moments of stillness.

### Phase 2: Inspiration

In literal terms, inspiration refers to the act of breathing in as well as denoting a state of being that is linked to 'unusual activity or creativity'.[1] When we are inspired, we feel infused with a vibrancy that fills our heart and mind with a sense of infinite possibility. This provides the perfect conditions for the seeds of creativity to germinate and grow.

Inspiration recharges us at the deepest levels and is fundamental to our ability to create and write. Connecting fully with this phase of the creative cycle requires us to be conscious of our individual sources of inspiration and include one or more in our daily life.

Inspiration may come from inner triggers at the level of our soul, which nudge us to follow intuitive impulses without knowing where they will lead. We may also be inspired by outer triggers like reading our favourite author's latest book or listening to music that boosts our mood.

Everyday tasks like cooking a meal can inspire us when approached with awareness, so feeding our family becomes a pleasure through using colourful ingredients and unusual flavours.

In addition to daily inspiration, punctuating our lives with experiences involving a more obvious break from our regular routine triggers our sense of adventure and leaves us feeling full of life. Spending the afternoon at an exhibition or the weekend at a festival recharges us creatively and injects fresh energy into our capacity for coming up with innovative ideas.

Once we embrace inspiration as an essential component of our creative path as Conscious Writers, we notice endless possibilities for wrapping our lives around it.

# Dive in

- Use a mind map or list-making process to come up with 20 sources of everyday and adventurous inspirational activities that resonate with you.

- Incorporate at least one in your daily life from this point on and ensure you include courageous choices on a regular basis.

- Schedule these in your diary now and continue doing so until regular inspiration becomes second nature and you no longer need the reminder.

## Phase 3: Imagination

The initial sparks of inspiration soon become the roaring flames of imagination when we encourage the process with our attention, awareness and action. Feeding the imagination provides fuel for expanding our ideas and enables us to play with potential like children, who have no difficulty with 'acting as if'.

We use our imagination to embellish the early prompting of our inspiration and come up with novel ways to shape the insights or tell the stories we're inspired to share. In fact, storytelling has long been associated with a rich use of the imagination. Characters come to life through recounting events that draw listeners or readers into imaginary worlds crafted from words. Thoreau went so far as to say, 'This world is but a canvas to our imagination.'

Entertainment and teaching through stories represents just one of many possible outlets for our boundless imagination. Einstein's view was that, 'Imagination is everything. It is the preview of life's coming attractions.' And Edgar Allen Poe suggested that, 'Those who dream by day are aware of many things which escape those who only dream by night.'

As with the sources of inspiration, there are countless possibilities for nourishing the magnificent gift of imagination we all have. Dipping into the rich forms our well-loved artists, musicians, poets and film directors have already created can greatly expand the boundaries of our own imagination. We just have to make it a priority on our way around the creative cycle in the knowledge that feeding our imagination is part of our creative development as Conscious Writers, not separate from it.

## Dive in

- Just for fun, imagine you have a magical power. What is it? How, when and where will you use it, and for what purpose?

- Set your imagination free and write on this until you feel done. Enjoy!

### Phase 4: Creative Expression

When the moment comes to express the essence of creativity fully in the world of form, our multi-layered preparation bears fruit from the seeds we've planted and the nurturing we've prioritized. As writers, this is the point at which our inspiration and imagination finally become words on the page and visible for us eventually to share with others.

We'll go more deeply into the writing process in Part III. For now, it's enough to realize that as one form of Conscious Creativity, Conscious Writing is a natural expression of our soul. When we align ourselves with that level of truth and nurture our ability to express it creatively, we discover a degree of inevitability and a sense of effortless flow.

That's not to say it's always easy. We still have to show up and remain present day after day to craft and create the forms that 'fit'. Nevertheless, when we're congruent with our soul and creatively charged, there's a subtle yet unmistakable Knowing that this is precisely what we're meant to be doing and somehow it will all come together in the end.

This phase of the cycle includes playing with forms and developing our creative muscles. Experimenting with a variety of creative options enriches our writing because all forms of creativity feed into each other. So, while we're focused on sculpting clay, a section of our book we've been struggling with suddenly falls into place.

Honouring our commitment to creative expression sometimes means simply giving ourselves permission to roll up our sleeves, get messy and have some creative fun!

## Dive in

- Think back to what you enjoyed doing creatively as a child. Include simple actions like cutting shapes into uncooked potatoes, painting the surface and creating a picture of coloured potato 'faces'.

- Research ideas for creative activities you've not tried before, like learning to draw a mandala or create stained-glass panels to play with colour and light. Download instructions from the internet or book yourself onto a workshop. Try your hand at something new.

- Write about your experiences, including how you felt before, during and after your creative play.

- Make it a priority once a week for the next month to enjoy different forms of creative expression without any requirement for an end result.

## Macro, Micro and Multi-layered

Our voyage around the creative cycle reveals the potential for igniting the fires of creative freedom as Conscious Writers. Yet, elegant though the connection between the creative and seasonal cycles may be, we may not always complete the circuit in one fell swoop.

At grassroots level we're likely to find ourselves weaving in and out of the different phases within the overall trajectory from phases 1 to 4. Just as warm, sunny days periodically punctuate winter and in the heat of summer we often need the cooling influence of stillness, our creative journey is unlikely to be a neat and tidy process of perpetual forward motion.

The uncertainty and chaos that are inherent aspects of creating anything new may lead us to return to silence after an initial idea arrives and open our hearts to receive deeper insight. It may be that only then are we ready to add imaginative detail and craft the final form of our creative expression.

In the early stages of developing an idea for example, a good question to ask our deep selves is, 'What do I actually mean by…?' or 'What does … truly mean to me?' Remaining still and allowing answers to arrive from our internal authentic space often opens up a new level of inspiration. This draws our imagination into the dance and triggers a cascade of fresh possibilities that enhance the original idea 100-fold.

The response to such questions may come in the form of words, phrases, images, sounds, feelings, or a combination of these echoes from the deep that guide us on our creative quest. Capturing the response with preliminary notes provides us with a visual component to reflect even greater clarity back to us from the page. From here, we may decide to drop back into phases 1, 2 or 3 before diving fully into our first draft flow.

Add to this the perspective of both macro and micro versions of the creative cycle and our view becomes ever more tempered on the anvil of experience. The whole process of writing a book can be seen as an immense progression over a period of time from initial stillness and inspired ideas through to developed detail and the completion of a final manuscript.

Yet the same creative phases are present at a much smaller scale when we focus on just one section, one page or one article for our blog. Connecting with each phase in succession can be almost instantaneous, and with awareness and practice we find ourselves ready to write in a matter of moments. Given the right conditions, the creative wheel will always turn.

## The Stages of Creativity

Students of creativity may wonder how the creative cycle relates to the stages of creativity as they are so often taught to artists and scientists alike. There are various theories on the number and sequence of the different stages relating to the creative process. One of the best-known derives from Graham Wallas who was a social psychologist, educationalist and contributing founder of the London School of Economics. In his book *The Art of Thought*, he proposed a theory that outlined four distinct stages:

1. *Preparation:* Deliberate activity directed towards investigating the problem and acquiring intellectual resources from which new ideas are constructed.

2. *Incubation:* Unconscious processing that requires relaxation or focus on something entirely separate to the problem being solved.

3. *Illumination:* Insight derived from the unconscious Incubation and earlier information gathered during Preparation.

4. *Verification:* Intentional effort exerted to validate the insight, implement the solution and manifest the product.[2]

These stages have certainly provided immensely valuable guidance, especially in the field of scientific discovery, since they were originally published in 1926. Yet Conscious Writing is not about solving problems in novel ways and we need to ensure that we understand the true depth required for fundamental creativity to occur.

The four stages are designed to trigger creativity from the conscious and unconscious workings of the mind, which is easily misinterpreted to mean the everyday mind. However, both quantum interpretation and spiritual insight reveal that the unconscious processing reaches a deeper level of truth.

Essentially, everything is an aspect of one whole and the everyday unconscious blends with the collective unconscious, which ultimately is an expression of 'Mind'. This is indeed the totality towards which we are pointing with our holistic approach to creativity. However, the terminology can become confusing unless we have an embodied sense of clarity around these matters, so distinguishing between everyday mind and true-self mind provides a more robust perspective for Conscious Writers.

Of course we can honour each phase of the creative cycle and apply the fruits of our experience to however many stages of creativity resonate with us as individuals. The creative cycle and stages of creativity are certainly not mutually exclusive. In fact it's a case of both/and as we discover the optimum conditions for our own creative expression.

When all is said and done, there are no absolute rules for developing a deep connection to creativity. Metaphors and staged processes are certainly useful to guide us initially, but ultimately our task is to set ourselves free to find a way that works for us and forge our own creative path.

Along the way, giving ourselves full permission to make time and space for connecting with each phase of the whole creative cycle provides us with a solid foundation on which to build our individual conscious and creative blend.

# PART III

*Experiencing
the Conscious
Writing Process*

# Expressing Your True Voice on the Page

As we make the final approach to the actual process of Conscious Writing, let's review all we've covered so far to enhance the perspective we take forwards to the page.

Conscious Writing is an invitation to realize our true nature, create what we're here to create and write what we're here to write.

The premise is that our state of consciousness determines and shapes the writing we do. As Conscious Writers, we prioritize inner preparation to shift beyond the usual identification we have with our everyday self, where our fears and anxieties lie. This opens the way for us to write creatively with full awareness from the level of our true self and the mystery beyond.

Conscious Writing is a journey of self-realization (conscious) and self-expression (creativity), which naturally leads us to discover our authentic voice on the page and in the world, and emerge transformed by the process. It's a way of writing that guides us to align all aspects of ourselves in order to bring our whole self to creative writing. Then we apply the outer skills of authorship relating to any and all types of writing and fluently blend soul with craft.

The holistic nature of Conscious Writing facilitates our access to the quantum realm of infinite potential, where we play with possibilities so our richest and most innovative ideas can be revealed. The essence finds form as words on the page that transmit to our readers a sense of the living reality towards which they point. This is the basis for our maximum contribution as writers who, in some small way, make a positive difference to people's lives. Along the way, we increasingly realize our full potential as authors – whatever that means for us as individuals.

Creating the right internal environment out of which deep writing flows freely comes from a commitment to becoming and remaining conscious. Seven core principles guide us towards personal experience of transpersonal Truth:

1.  *Presence* – draws us into the Now where we explore the infinite potential of awareness beyond the mind.

2.  *Alignment* – affirms that when we reach beyond head and heart to include body and soul we access the deepest levels of conscious and creative flow.

3.  *Authenticity* – lines up our inner true self with our outer everyday self and creates space for our authentic voice to be discovered and shared.

4.  *Balance* – reminds us of the importance of both focus and flow in the dance of creation and the pinnacle point of riding the creative wave when both are present.

5.  *Simplicity* – allows what is truly important to rise effortlessly to the surface and reveals what genuinely makes our heart sing.

6.  *Intuition* – guides us to follow the golden threads of inner impulses and outer inspirations to Know that we're on track with our primary purpose.

7.  *Connection* – leads us to blend the individual narrative with the universal story for the greater good of all as we inhabit the wholeness of which we are an integral part.

Taking forwards the awareness we've cultivated enables us to dive in deeply to creative flow and our conscious 'in-breath' becomes the creative 'out-breath' of our writing and our life. We learn to live the questions of our creative enquiry and embrace the mystery as we work towards increasing alignment with the process of Creation. Releasing the limitations of conditioning and belief, we forge new pathways and craft an expanded vision. Inspired by nature, we nurture our creative soul and commit to sustaining our output for the whole duration as the wheel turns, stillness inspires and imagination creates.

Finally we see, once and for all, that honouring the 90 per cent below the surface of the water is just what the tip of the iceberg requires. Our dedication is rewarded at every level as our words find their way into the hearts and minds of our readers, and we live the truth of our conscious and creative calling.

CHAPTER 11

# TWO ADDITIONAL COMPONENTS

I fell in love with Bali within 24 hours of arriving, the same time-frame it took for me to travel from the wilds of Wiltshire in south-west England to this Indonesian 'island of the gods'. Weary from the long journey but excited finally to have reached my destination, I met the intense heat and dark night with an open heart. My body was rewarded with an ice-cold scented flannel, a refreshing juice and an exquisite garland of flowers. The beauty of my surroundings was surpassed only by the exceptional warmth of the Balinese people, whose elegance and grace overflowed through smiling faces.

The next morning I awoke to the majesty of lush tropical gardens leading directly onto the beach. Richly coloured flowers framed the snaking paths and I was greeted by the fragrance of frangipani and the sound of water falling gently into a clear pool where brightly coloured fish were swimming freely. The breakfast feast included the sweetest of melons, the freshest pineapple, and fruits I had never even seen before, let alone tried! The steaming green tea was a perfect complement to my journal-writing session and my words poured enthusiastically onto the page as I took stock of the amazing start to my latest adventure.

This was just the beginning of what was to become one of the most memorable and transformative multi-sensory experiences of my life so far. The central focus of the trip was a week-long yoga pranala retreat that was being held at a beautiful location in the heart of the jungle just outside Ubud, the main cultural centre. After a few days at the coast, where my love of nature, colour, scent, beauty and elegance was validated like never before, I made my way inland to prepare for my intense week of yoga and spiritual development.

## Yoga Pranala

Yoga pranala is an original blend of yoga *asanas* (postures), *pranayama* (breath control), meditation and *mudra pranala*, which is a form of Balinese *qi gong* and energy movement to open the heart and connect with divine consciousness. This combination was created by experienced yoga teacher Linda Madani, who has been a student of renowned and respected Balinese healer and shaman Tjokorda Rai since 1996.[1]

The grandson of the last king of Ubud, Tjokorda Rai lives in the royal compound of Puri Negari, where he combines traditional healing techniques with contemporary application. Despite being in his early eighties, he has legendary energy and charisma, and he is visited daily by streams of Balinese people and tourists who are looking for answers to health issues of every kind. His vast knowledge and wisdom are tempered with humility, a broad smile and a distinct sparkle in his eye. In addition to his work as a healer, he also emphasizes development through the balance of opposites and teaches his own system of mudras, which are gestures and movements to balance mind and body, called *pranala*.

Linda Madani has incorporated these energy techniques and mudras into her teaching of yoga, with Tjokorda Rai's blessing, and as soon as I learned of this unique combination, I knew that this would be a perfect retreat for me. It closely reflected the different facets of my existing practice and would introduce me to new ways of working with energy Balinese-style that I was keen to discover. When I found out that I would also have the chance to meet Tjokorda Rai, experience one of his healing sessions and participate in a sacred Balinese ceremony at the end of the retreat, the decision to attend was made in an instant!

During our highly focused time together, Linda taught the mudra sequence that was an integral part of the final ceremony. Interestingly, it felt strangely familiar and had a particularly powerful impact on me, which, combined with the other components of the ritual, served to complete a major shift within me that remains permanent to this day.

Understandably, we were sworn to secrecy in relation to that particular mudra sequence, given the in-depth nature of the original teaching from Tjokorda Rai and the sacred oral tradition he upholds. However, it touched such a deep place within me that I was inspired to create my own equivalent following my intuitive inner guidance.

A few months later, once the integration of my experience was complete, I developed a simple contemporary version of this ancient practice for sharing with others through the Conscious Writing process. The intention was to facilitate a relatively rapid transition from the everyday world to the presence and alignment required for Conscious Writing to serve writers living busy modern lives. As a result, short windows of writing time would become just as productive as longer stretches of creative immersion.

It is deeply rewarding to have discovered just how well this process actually works for people in practice, and we'll come to the detail of the mudra sequence and the whole Conscious Writing process in Chapter 12. In the meantime, let's take a closer look at mudras as the first of the two additional components that form part of the Conscious Writing process.

## Mudras and More

*Mudra* is a Sanskrit word meaning 'seal' or 'gesture' and refers to sacred and symbolic gestures, usually of the hands and fingers.

Mudras are used in many traditions, including Buddhism, Hinduism, Taoism and Tantra, for ritual, ceremonies and classical dance. In yoga, they are often combined with *pranayama* (breath control) to affect the practitioner in different ways, including the flow of *prana* (life force) in the body. In spiritual practice and meditation generally, mudras are used to facilitate access to states of consciousness beyond the everyday level we usually experience.

There are hundreds of mudras which can be performed with either one or two hands and which sometimes have complicated and esoteric interpretations. The *hasta-mudras* of Hindu classical dance, for example, can express 500 different meanings.[2]

In the Vedic tradition, the physical body is understood to be made up of five elements – air, water, fire, earth and *akasha* (ether) – and these correspond to the five digits on each hand:

- *Thumb*   Fire
- *Index*   Air
- *Middle*   Akasha
- *Ring*   Earth
- *Little*   Water

When the elements are in balance, we experience health. When they are out of balance, the immune system is disrupted, which can cause disease. Balance of the elements can be restored through the practice of mudras which trigger electromagnetic currents within the body and in due course return the system to health.[3]

The hands also have many reflex points that connect to specific parts of the mind and body through *nadis*, or energy channels. By shaping our hands in precise ways, such as touching the fingertips, stretching or curling the fingers, or clasping the hands together, we can send messages to direct the flow of energy in the body. This revitalizes and supports our health and wellbeing at every level.[4]

One of the best-known mudras is the Guyan Mudra, where the tip of the thumb (universal consciousness) touches the tip of the index finger (individual consciousness) and the other fingers are extended. The connection of thumb and index finger symbolizes the union of the individual with universal consciousness.

*Figure 6: The Guyan Mudra*

The Guyan Mudra is often taught for meditation with the palms facing upwards to open the heart centre and is used to induce a calm, receptive state for receiving peace, wisdom and spiritual awareness.

Mudras are often performed in a sequence. The following series of four mudras is drawn from kundalini yoga for balancing energy.[5]

# Dive in

- Use both hands and alternately touch the tips of each finger with the tip of your thumb. Maintain the connection for a few seconds or until it feels appropriate to move on to the next finger.

- The individual hand positions also have specific effects as follows:

*Figure 7: Thumb to Tip of Index Finger: energy into the legs and lower body and induces a sense of calm and concentration.*

*Figure 8: Thumb to Tip of Middle Finger: promotes patience.*

*Figure 9: Thumb to Tip of Ring Finger: encourages energy, stability and self-confidence plus constancy of the physical experience and sturdiness within the body.*

*Figure 10: Thumb to Tip of Little Finger: enhances intuition and feeling, and gives a sense of freshness to the mind and body.*

Interestingly, research has demonstrated that hand gestures stimulate the same region of the brain as language, which suits our purposes as Conscious Writers perfectly.[6]

## NLP Anchoring

An alternative way of understanding how specific gestures have the potential to effect changes in our state of consciousness is the technique of anchoring used in neuro-linguistic programming (NLP).

An anchor is 'an internal state that is triggered by an external stimulus'. 'Anchoring' is the term that describes the process of applying 'a gesture, touch or sound at the peak of a state' to associate that state with the chosen stimulus. Once the anchor is created and reinforced by repeated stimuli, the state can be instantly reactivated by reapplying the stimulus.[7]

This technique is similar to classical conditioning. In 1904, the Russian physiologist Ivan Pavlov won the Nobel Prize for Physiology or Medicine – disciplines to which he'd dedicated his life's work – yet he is best known for one particular study involving the salivary secretions in dogs.

Pavlov's research involved observing the stimuli that triggered salivation, including actually putting food in the animal's mouth. Over time, he noticed that working with the same dog repeatedly caused salivation to begin when the dog saw items associated with food, such as the person who delivered it and the dish in which it was presented. This revealed a specific kind of learning: 'An involuntary action (salivation) that is usually triggered only by a certain class of events (food) was now being controlled by a new stimulus (the sight of the experimenter).'

As the study progressed, Pavlov experimented with using a neutral stimulus that didn't initially cause the dog to salivate – the sound of a bell – just before delivering food. With just a few repetitions of this sequence, the bell, which had not affected the dog originally, caused the dog to salivate. It became apparent that the neutral stimulus could be anything at all and still create the same effect. Obviously this wasn't happening through the dog's active participation, yet worked nevertheless.[8]

Anchoring reflects the same process at work. As Conscious Writers, we can learn to create and use anchors consciously for a wide range of purposes. These include triggering positive feelings of competence in relation to writing and all the actions required of us as published authors.

Yet it's also useful to realize that anchors are created unconsciously as part of everyday life. The more awareness we have around these automatic associations, the more we can benefit from this natural tendency we all have.

As an example, each year I nurture my creative soul by attending a fabulous festival of music, arts and dance that is held in the most glorious setting of gardens and woodland. This year, I discovered a new artist called Ivan Hussey, who is a highly skilled cellist and the front man for the band Celloman. He played a Sunday afternoon set of songs from his album *Moods, Broods and Interludes* with just one fellow musician on violin.[9] The sun was shining brightly and I had a refreshing glass of crisp Chardonnay to complement the inspirational melodies these master musicians were playing. The whole experience was so uplifting that I bought the CD afterwards. Now, each time I listen to it, not only am I taken back to the scene but also to the *feeling* of that sunny afternoon. I hadn't planned this association intentionally – it just happened naturally and an anchor was created.

Clearly then, with awareness and conscious intention, we can create anchors to support all aspects of our work as Conscious Writers, and the mudra sequence we learn as part of the Conscious Writing process serves precisely that purpose.

There's a great deal of information available about anchoring from experts in NLP. They explain the subtleties and nuances of this technique, but the basic process for establishing an anchor is to:

- Select a specific state you want to trigger, such as confidence.

- Bring to mind the memory of a time when you felt supremely confident, or, if necessary, imagine what it would feel like as vividly as you possibly can.

- When you have recreated the feelings of confidence, make a specific gesture, touch or sound to establish the anchor.

- Repeat the process several times so that you learn to associate the anchor you've chosen with the state of confidence.

- Thereafter, you'll be able to activate the anchor by using the gesture, touch or sound to trigger feeling confident.

As with all such suggestions and techniques, you'll only know the benefits for yourself after personal experience, so dive in and play with these possibilities to enhance the results of your Conscious Writing experience.

# Visualization

The second of the two additional components that form part of the Conscious Writing process is visualization, another ancient spiritual practice that has been adapted for use in the modern world.

The practice of visualization dates back to early Babylonian and Egyptian times, and is found in many of the world's spiritual philosophies, including Hindu, Tantra and Tibetan Buddhism. Thousands of years ago, Greek philosopher and scientist Aristotle realized that thinking involved imagery and taught that they were essential companions in relation to motivation. Since then, many great thinkers have been equally inspired by the potential of visualization as an effective technique that can be successfully applied to many different areas of life.

Visualization is essentially the process of using mental imagery to support the attainment of specific intentions. American businessman Bo Bennett described it as 'daydreaming with a purpose'.

We've already seen how significant our mind is when it comes to creating our experience of life. Gautama Buddha reminds us that, 'The mind is everything; what you think, you become.' From here, it only requires a small additional step to appreciate the potential of using our imagination and inner senses to instruct our mind and body to function in specific ways for optimum results.

Over recent years, a great deal of research has been done which has shown that the brain doesn't distinguish between doing something 'for real' and imagining doing it.

Studies using brain imagery have revealed that:

> *'...visualization works because neurons in our brains, those electrically excitable cells that transmit information, interpret imagery as equivalent to a real-life action. When we visualize an act, the brain generates an impulse that tells our neurons to "perform" the movement. This creates a new neural pathway – clusters of cells in our brain that work together to create memories or learned behaviours – that primes our body to act in a way consistent to what we imagined. All of this occurs without actually performing the physical activity, yet it achieves a similar result.'*[10]

One well-documented study was done in 1994 at the Harvard Medical School, where two groups of volunteers were involved in what was known as 'The Piano Study'. Members of the first group were instructed by neuroscientist Alvaro Pascual-Leone to play a simple five-finger piano exercise each day for five days. They were then tested using transcranial magnetic stimulation (TMS) to assess the function of neurons and how much of the motor cortex controlling the finger movements was used in the exercise.

The second group was asked simply to imagine playing the same piano exercise over the same period of time, without any physical movement of the fingers. The results showed that the region of the motor cortex that controlled the piano-playing fingers expanded to virtually the same extent in *both* groups. This proved that thought and imagination could alter the physical structure and function of the brain.[11]

Visualization is now widely used to enhance performance and improve success in a variety of disciplines. At the highest levels in sport, for example, tennis star Billie Jean King used visualization effectively from the 1960s onwards, and numerous Olympic athletes receive instruction from sports psychologists, who now form an integral part of the team. Incorporating mental imagery and rehearsal into training regimes builds confidence and benefits physical movement while also increasing the power of concentration and decreasing the impact of pressure related to competing.

## Creative Visualization

In the creative realms, Walt Disney was well known for believing in the power of visualization, which he called 'imagineering', and the actor Jim Carrey used creative visualization successfully on his way to stardom. He wrote himself a 10-million-dollar cheque 'for acting services rendered' in 1987 and dated it 'Thanksgiving 1995'. He then visualized his goal for many years before finally achieving it in 1994 for his role in the film *Dumb and Dumber.*[12]

Creative visualization is usually focused on harnessing the power of imagination to produce positive change. Oprah Winfrey states, 'I do believe, and I have seen in my own life, that creative visualization works,' and Rosabeth Moss Kanter, who is a professor of business at Harvard Business School, adds, 'A vision is not just a picture of what could be; it is an appeal to our better selves, a call to become something more.'

Such an approach can indeed call forth a positive attitude in relation to the vision we have of ourselves as writers and support us in developing the attributes we need to succeed as authors. We can also visualize ourselves writing freely without judgement and use imagery to infuse our words with colour and depth so the worlds we create in our imagination are portrayed more vividly on the page. We may create a mental image of our readers to sharpen our focus of who we are writing for and then allow this to guide us when we reach out to connect with our audience. With regard to marketing and promotion, visualization could be just what we need to build our confidence for book signings and readings, as well as the speaking engagements and media interviews that will spread the word about our book's availability.

However, as with everything, the state of consciousness we bring to the process of creative visualization is crucial. When we're caught up in the ego-based desires of the everyday self, which usually involve an exclusive degree of personal gain, we risk losing a sense of the big picture and missing unforeseen opportunities.

In order to avoid the drawbacks of the mundane perspective the everyday self usually has, we need to ensure that we're consciously aligned with our true self when setting our intentions for creative visualization. From here, we are free to visualize positive outcomes for our creative endeavours without being excessively attached to specific results. This approach leaves room for delightful surprises to occur that serve the greater good of all concerned, including ourselves.

# Dive in

Give yourself permission to dive in and explore this technique, which can be applied to any aspect of writing and authorship.

- Begin by acting as if visualization will work for you, even if you don't yet have any evidence to support that. Remember, if you approach this believing it's unlikely to make any difference, you'll undoubtedly prove yourself right! Remind yourself of the scientific evidence we've covered in this chapter, if that helps initially.

- Relax your body and focus on your breathing for a few minutes to quieten your mind and facilitate the expansion of your awareness beyond the matters of everyday life.

- Reflect deeply on the intention you'd like to set for your creative visualization practice, such as developing a daily writing rhythm, feeling confident about sharing your work with others or speaking with authority during an interview.

- Create a mental image of a successful outcome to the intention you've chosen and include as much detail and clarity as possible. In your mind's eye, see the image becoming larger and brighter.

- When you feel ready, take an imaginary step into the image so you become the person and see the environment from within it rather than seeing it on a movie screen in your mind.

- Add sensory components such as sounds and textures as well as thoughts and feelings that realistically reflect the fruitful effects you're aiming for. *Feel* the certainty that arises from being in the flow and on track with your purpose, and remain in the scene for as long as it feels right to do so.

- Repeat the visualization process as often as possible, including at odd moments during the day such as when you're waiting for the kettle to boil. Immerse yourself in the experience.

- In addition, take appropriate action to support the process of your intentions becoming your reality. It's not enough to imagine your intended outcome and sit back in your chair waiting for it to fall into your lap!

If seeing images in your mind's eye doesn't come easily, you can still benefit from this technique by learning to perceive your inner world in a way that works for you. Studying photos then closing your eyes and recalling as much detail as you can may help to sharpen your inner vision. Alternatively you can focus on developing your other inner senses by thinking of a lemon and imagine touching the surface of its skin, cutting it open and smelling the citrus scent and tasting the zesty flavour. Include the thoughts and feelings associated with slicing a lemon to practise combining your inner senses in a way that will serve your intended purpose when you apply it to the creative outcome you're aiming for.

## Guided Visualization

Guided visualization is an extension of everything we've covered so far on visualization with the addition of receiving external instruction, either from another person or an audio CD that's been created for the purpose, which literally guides the process at every level.

With guided visualization, we are directed to see and sense specific details, which often include a basic narrative such as a simple journey from one inner space to another where we access optimum capacities for addressing our intentions. Scripts for guided visualization can be created for all purposes, including healing, relaxation and personal development.

The Conscious Writing process includes a guided visualization that we will come to in the next chapter. It draws on the immense potential of using imagery to support us in connecting with the conscious awareness we've been exploring and in reaching a deep creative space within ourselves before we write.

The inner space we visit is called the Conscious Writing Sanctuary, and it can be used for a multitude of purposes, including finding inner peace and focus when our outer environment doesn't provide us with those ideal conditions. Combined with the other components of the Conscious Writing process, it provides us with access to realms beyond the everyday so we can write from our heart with the voice of our soul.

Some of the comments received from writers after experiencing this process for the very first time include:

- *'Brilliant – just what I needed. It opened up material for the book I've been sitting on for 10+ years! Excellent on every level.'*

- *'Within a short time I had connected with a deeper part of my creative self that I hadn't even known was there. My creative energy was surging through me; I felt I was riding a wave.'*

- *'I feel blessed to have been shown the way to connect with my deeper self and write from my heart.'*

- *'I am truly inspired – a very profound experience. Touched me on a deep level, and I was amazed at how much my writing flowed.'*

We'll visit the Conscious Writing Sanctuary in the next chapter and gain first-hand experience of the tremendous potential it has to offer for developing our ideas and finding the right words to express them.

# CHAPTER 12

# VISITING THE CONSCIOUS WRITING SANCTUARY

The next level of the journey begins here. Having examined the individual pieces of the Conscious Writing jigsaw, it's now time to see the picture they collectively create. The preparation is complete. The moment has come to write. Let's dive straight in.

## Overview

The Conscious Writing process begins with five phases of alignment:

1.  Physical movement to wake up the body and stimulate the flow of energy. You will learn the process with skeletal shaking, but feel free to experiment over time with different kinds of physical activity such as walking or yoga in advance of the other components.

2.  Deep, conscious breathing to flood your whole system with vitality.

3.  The mudra sequence to ground and expand your awareness beyond the everyday.

4.  Full relaxation to release tension and shift your brain into alpha mode to activate feelings of calm, confidence and clarity.

5.  Open positive emotions like happiness, joy and love, which trigger feel-good hormones, to strengthen your capacity for positive self-belief and more.

These phases of alignment lead directly to the guided visualization that takes you on the inner journey to the Conscious Writing Sanctuary. This is a safe and secure internal space where you have full permission to express yourself without censorship or judgement. Once you arrive, you are instructed to pick up your writing tools and write until you feel ready to stop. Alternatively, you can set a timer for 20 or 30 minutes – or more – and wrap up the writing when the time is done. At this point, you put your writing tools down and complete the guided visualization, going back to where you started your inner journey.

Ideally, you'll have some time and space directly after your Conscious Writing process for sitting quietly to reflect on your experience and allow whatever has arisen to settle within you before resuming everyday activities.

The guided visualization script is included here and you can work with it in a number of ways:

- You can read it aloud and record it on any device such as a smart phone or bespoke voice recorder. Do two separate recordings: one to take you up to the point where you do your writing and one to complete your journey afterwards.

- A trusted friend, writing buddy or fellow member of a Conscious Writing Circle (*see page 192*) can read the script aloud for you to follow and guide you through the whole process.

- You can purchase the CD or download the MP3 of the official *Conscious Writing: The Process* audio, which includes music and more to enhance your Conscious Writing experience (*see page 191*).

Sufficient repetitions of the process will eventually allow you to make the journey to your inner Conscious Writing Sanctuary without external prompting by simply following the path you have come to know, and hopefully to love, through extended experience with the guided version.

Before we begin, I would like to honour two additional sources of inspiration and teaching that have enabled me to create the Conscious Writing process in the way that I have. The late Dr Glenn Morris was the originator of a kundalini awakening process which was taught to me some years ago by yogi, teacher and author Tao Semko. With Tao's immense knowledge and experience, I received skilful direction that led me to discover new realms of possibility for working consciously with energy, and a great deal more besides. It is with respect and gratitude that I acknowledge Tao's clarity and specific suggestions alongside general guidance that provided the foundation on which I have built the Conscious Writing process.[1]

# Dive in

Have your writing tools – pen and paper or laptop – nearby and choose a location that is away from your usual workspace. You can use a different part of the same room or go somewhere else entirely. Ensure that you won't be disturbed for the duration of your Conscious Writing experience.

## 1.   Set Your Intention

Choose one of the following options and write your choice down in your Conscious Writing Journal or at the top of the paper you've set aside for your writing:

- Leave it open and see what arises spontaneously while asking for whatever you need at this time to show up on the page.

- Develop your ideas for a new or existing topic that's in the early stages of creative unfolding.

- Set a clear intention to write the first draft of a blog post or a specific section of the book you're currently working on.

## 2.   Stretch and Breathe

Stand up, take a deep breath in, and as you do so, stretch your arms up to the sky above you, as far as you can reach. As you breathe out, sweep your fingertips lightly down the front of your body as you exhale, releasing a 'haaa' sound from your mouth. This movement symbolizes clearing the space within you for creative inspiration to flow. Repeat this a few times.

## 3.   Skeletal Shaking

Shake your body with slow to moderate movements that have a downward focus. Shake your hands and arms, your feet and your legs, and include your whole body, to loosen your muscles and stimulate the flow of energy from the top of your head to the tip of your toes.

Deepen your breathing naturally with the movement and drop your awareness into your body to *feel* the energy as much as you are able to at this time. Harness the aptitude of your sensory awareness to notice warmth or tingling or similar sensations that are particular to how you experience the feeling of energy flowing within you.

This 'skeletal shaking' supports you in feeling grounded, strengthens bone density and cultivates the flow of *qi*, or life force, within you.

## 4.    Stand

Now come to rest in a standing position with your feet shoulder-width apart and your arms hanging loosely by your sides. Elongate your spine, soften your knees and just stand still with your weight evenly distributed on your feet, balanced and at ease. Close your eyes or rest your gaze lightly on the floor just a short way in front of you.

## 5.    Deepen Your Breath

Consciously deepen your breath and place your hands lightly on the lower part of your belly, just below the navel. Breathe in and out and feel your belly expand with the in-breath and contract back towards your spine with the out-breath. Aim for the out-breath to be twice as long as the in-breath. Don't strain in any way, and once you've established a comfortable rhythm, allow your arms to hang loosely by your sides once more.

Our breath connects every aspect of ourselves. When we deepen our breathing, we oxygenate our blood, which nourishes the physical body and has a calming effect on the mind and emotions.

## 6.    The Mudra Sequence

Imagine that you have roots like a tree which emerge from the soles of your feet and reach deep into the earth beneath you. In the native wisdom traditions, this is Mother Earth, the Divine Feminine. Send your awareness into the earth and connect with the ultimate creative principle. Feel grounded and confident.

At the same time, leaving your arms hanging by your sides, turn your palms to a horizontal position, facing the earth beneath your feet (*see Figure 11*).

*Figure 11: Mudra Sequence: palms down.*

Draw your awareness back up through your body and imagine that you have branches emerging from the upper part of your body reaching high up to the sky above you, just like the tallest of trees. In the native wisdom traditions, this is Father Sky, the Divine Masculine. Send your awareness into the sky and connect with the ultimate guiding principle. Feel focused and strong.

Simultaneously, turn your palms upwards to face the sky above your head. (*See Figure 12*)

*Figure 12: Mudra Sequence: palms up.*

Now, leaving your right palm as it is, return your left palm to the original position facing downwards to the earth beneath you. (*See Figure 13*) Feel the feminine and masculine energies both flowing through you.

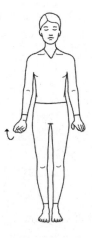

*Figure 13: Mudra Sequence: left palm down, right palm up.*

When you feel ready, on your next in-breath bend your arms and bring your palms up to the level of your heart, where you turn the left palm back up so you have both palms facing upwards at the level of your heart. (*See Figure 14*)

*Figure 14: Mudra Sequence: hands to heart level, both palms up.*

Continue with the in-breath and raise your arms and hands into a 'V' shape above your head. Look up in this primal open-hearted gesture. Pause here for a moment. (*See Figure 15*)

*Figure 15: Mudra Sequence: arms up to 'V' shape, open your heart.*

Now bring your palms together above your head. Then drop your chin to return your gaze to the front or close your eyes once more. (*See Figure 16*)

*Figure 16: Mudra Sequence: palms together above your head; then gaze forwards or close your eyes.*

On the next out-breath, draw both palms – and the energy with them – down to your third eye area and feel the feminine and masculine energies dancing together and blending into one ecstatic whole. (*See Figure 17*)

*Figure 17: Mudra Sequence: draw palms and energy down to your third eye area.*

Breathe in and out once more, and as you do so, bring your palms, along with the blended energies, back down to the level of your heart in a traditional prayer position. Rest here for a moment and breathe deeply. (*See Figure 18*)

*Figure 18: Mudra Sequence: return palms to prayer position in front of your heart.*

### 7.   Take Your Seat

Now sit down comfortably on the edge of your chair with your feet shoulder-width apart and flat on the floor and your spine straight. Rest your hands lightly on your thighs with your palms facing down.

### 8.   Relax Your Body

Deepen the relaxation of your body further by initially tightening all of your muscles intentionally for a count of three and then releasing the tension as you breathe out with your mouth open while you actively let go. Repeat this a few times.

Imagine that your body is hollow and feel as if it's being filled with a warm wave of liquid light that begins at the tip of your toes and spreads up through your whole body, rising up your legs, your hips, and torso, flooding into your arms and hands, spreading across your shoulders, melting any tension it meets along the way, and finally rising up through your neck, face and all the way to the crown of your head. Expand your awareness to sense that your whole body is warm, relaxed and filled with light.

### 9.   Open Positive Emotion

Now place your hands on your heart and remember a time when you felt truly happy. This could be the memory of an experience you shared with family or friends, a special time with a favourite animal or simply the joy at seeing a beautiful flower. The details aren't important, it's the feeling that counts, so feel the feeling and flood your body with joy and love. Bring a natural smile to your face as this will add to the feel-good hormones in your system. Immerse yourself in joy and let it flood into every cell of your body.

### 10.   Surrender to the Flow

Settle into those feelings of joy and return your hands to rest gently on your thighs with your palms facing down. The journey is about to begin…

## Guided Visualization: The Path to the Conscious Writing Sanctuary

*In your mind's eye, you are now standing on a beach looking out over the ocean. The sand is soft and white. The sea is calm and a brilliant turquoise.*

*You feel the warmth of a hot sun overhead seeping through you and relaxing you even more deeply as you let go of the everyday world.*

*There's a gentle breeze blowing and you feel inspired to turn and walk across the sand away from the sea. Feel the sand shifting underneath your feet as you walk.*

*The sand gradually gives way to grassy dunes and ahead you see a lush green meadow. A narrow meandering path crosses the meadow and you begin to walk along it, enjoying the feelings of freedom that are triggered by being in this beautiful place.*

*On either side of the path you enjoy the array of wild and wonderful flowers of all shapes, sizes and colours – red and purple, yellow and white.*

*As you continue, a little further on you see a wood with a high mountain beyond. Following the path takes you into the wood. The sun is shining through the trees, casting a dappled light on the path, and you delight in a carpet of bluebells to your right and left underneath the trees. You hear birds singing and pick up the faint scent of this rich and timeless woodland.*

*Eventually the path takes you to a large circular clearing. The open space is illuminated by the sun's rays and as you walk into the clearing, you see a pool of crystal-clear water over to your right.*

*As you walk towards the pool, you notice a large tree just beyond it. This is the Wisdom Tree. You discover a seat at the base of the trunk and feel drawn to sit down. Instantly you realize that the seat fits you perfectly, as if it has been made just for you.*

*The beauty and stillness are captivating, and you are mesmerized by the dancing reflections on the surface of the water as the sunlight glistens and sparkles like diamonds. You sense that this is a magical pool as the world of reflections beckons you and begins to offer glimpses of truth, insights and ideas. These may not be sharp and clear initially, but in time you will understand what is being communicated and know that whatever it is, it will be what is most important for you to be aware of at this time.*

*As you allow the reflections to permeate through you, something glints in the sunshine and catches your eye down by your feet. You see that it is a dazzling raw crystal. Now you notice that there are many beautiful crystals all around.*

*You pick one up and intuitively know that you can hold it, set an intention and then throw it into the pool to receive insight on anything you like.*

*With the raw crystal in your hand, take a moment to set your intention or request for insight now.*

*[Pause.]*

*When you've filled the raw crystal with your intention, gently throw it into the shimmering water.*

*Watch the ripples the crystal makes and let your mind rest easily in the emptiness, feeling no requirement to grasp for ideas or answers. Instead, simply open your heart and invite whatever you need to arise as you write.*

*You feel calm, confident and deeply creative as the energy bubbles up inside you on its way to the surface of your conscious awareness.*

*In a moment, in the physical world, you will open your eyes, pick up your writing tools and begin to write. Retain the image in your mind's eye of sitting next to the pool while you write and know that your writing doesn't have to be anything other than whatever appears on the page at this time. Let it flow and write freely, without judgement.*

*Pick up your writing tools and begin your writing now...*

## Completing the Visualization

*It's now time to leave the Conscious Writing Sanctuary, the safe and welcoming inner space that you've created for your writing.*

*Before you do so, give thanks for whatever gifts you've received today, even if you aren't yet sure what they are. They may show up later, or in a few days' time. Be alert for the magic to continue working long after you've left this sacred creative space.*

*For now, take your leave and go back the same way you came. Leave the comfortable seat in the Wisdom Tree and take one last look at the reflections in the pool. You feel relaxed and renewed, ready to return to the everyday world, enriched by your experience.*

*You turn and make your way across the clearing and pick up the path back through the wood ... you continue your journey across the beautiful meadow ... and the grassy dunes ... over the white sand ... all the way back to the edge of the ocean, returning to where you started.*

*Pause here for a moment to let your experience settle within you.*

*When you are ready, take a deep breath, open your eyes and rejoin the everyday world. Rest in stillness for a while before moving and know that you can visit your Conscious Writing Sanctuary whenever you choose to do so.*

# Quick Summary

When you're familiar with the process from having followed the detailed instructions a number of times, the following quick summary will be enough to remind you of the order the alignment phases take prior to the guided visualization:

1.  Set your intention.

2.  Stretch and breathe.

3.  Skeletal shaking.

4.  Stand.

5.  Deepen your breath.

6.  The mudra sequence:
    *   Roots – palms down.
    *   Branches – palms up.
    *   Left palm down, right palm up.
    *   Hands to heart level, both palms up.
    *   Arms up to 'V' shape – open the heart.
    *   Palms together above your head, look up; then gaze forwards or close your eyes.
    *   Draw palms and energy down to the third eye area.
    *   Return palms to prayer position in front of the heart.

7.  Take your seat.

8.  Relax your body.

9.  Open positive emotion.

10. Surrender to the flow.

11. Begin the guided visualization ... write.

12. Complete the guided visualization and pause before resuming regular activities.

This tried-and-tested process has enabled writers to transition from everyday life into creative writing mode quickly and effectively while opening the way for deep insights and original ideas to take shape on the page, often in delightful and unexpected ways.

My invitation to you is to dive in and experience the rewards of the Conscious Writing process for yourself, and repeat as required to complete the writing you're here to do.

⌣

CHAPTER 13

# Conscious Writing at Every Stage

In the last chapter we saw how the different components of the Conscious Writing process work together and can be applied to the preliminary stages of developing ideas and first-draft writing. Yet this process has the potential to make a positive difference to *all* stages of writing and authorship as it leads us to take skilful action in the outer world from a strong foundation of inner congruence. As a result, the insights and qualities we need to succeed become more readily available to us as we find our own combination of soul and craft.

## The Stages of Writing

Opinions vary regarding the number of stages involved in the process of writing. They range from three to a dozen, depending on the way the contents of each stage are distributed and whether or not publishing is included.

Given the emphasis we place in Conscious Writing on the importance of inner preparation, it's no surprise to discover that this is the first of five stages we go through as Conscious Writers:

1. Preparation.

2. Inspiration.

3. First draft.

4. Refine and revise.

5. Edit and complete.

Just as we saw with the creative cycle, these stages don't necessarily follow a neat linear progression. Preparation leads to inspiration and first-draft writing, although during the early phases of inspiration we may dip regularly back into preparation before a single word meets the page. The first draft will always require refinement and revision, yet this may end up being more of a dance to and fro than a clear-cut boundary between one and the other. A great deal depends on the nature of the content, the relationship we have with it and our optimum way of working.

For our purposes here, exploring each stage in the typical order enables us to appreciate the subtlety and detail of the creative framework as well as the potential contribution the Conscious Writing process can make to each one.

## Stage 1: Preparation

The initial invitation to dip a toe in the waters of Conscious Writing has already led us through a significant degree of preparation. We began by meeting the 'conscious' in Conscious Writing and learning how to work with the seven core principles that support us to become and remain conscious. From here, we opened a deep flow on the voyage through creativity, where releasing conditioned patterns of thought and behaviour paved the way for nurturing our creative soul to manifest our true creative vision. Gathering all of this together led us into the Conscious Writing process, which can be understood as a bridge between the inner world of possibility and the outer world of actuality.

Let's just remind ourselves *why* we engage in this amount of preparation. In *Henry V*, Shakespeare wrote, 'All things are ready, if our mind be so.' With Conscious Writing, we ready the mind with an initial inner focus that enables us to write from the level of our true self and the mystery beyond to bypass the fears and anxieties of the everyday self. This in turn opens the way for us to realize our full potential as authors and stand out from the crowd by making a truly authentic contribution with our work.

The question 'Why?' is also the first of two additional areas of reflection that form part of the preparation stage. I invite you to use the Conscious Writing process to delve into genuine clarity in relation to both of these questions, starting with…

## 1. Why?

Knowing *why* you want to write is a key component of your vision of authorship. It serves to create a clear intention at every level that supports you in prioritizing your actions, staying on track when challenges arise and making appropriate decisions along the way.

Clarifying your 'Why?' involves diving deeply into your motivation for writing your book, your blog and the other materials you're here to write. By way of example, here's an edited version of my reflections prior to writing this book:

- *Motivation:* I am following a strong inner impulse and Conscious Writing is one lens through which the essence of Truth can pour into the world – via my work and the contribution that Conscious Writers everywhere have the potential to make.

- *My objective* is for the book to reach the widest possible international audience and make a positive difference in the lives of aspiring and published Conscious Writers and readers.

- *Outcome:* I aim to write a book that resonates deeply with Truth at every level – each word, phrase, sentence, paragraph, section, chapter and as a whole. I intend the content to flow effortlessly onto the page and into a clear structure presenting inspired insights for people who are interested in this holistic approach to writing and authorship.

# Dive in

Now it's your turn. Draw on the vision of creativity you crafted (*from the practice on page 137*) and set the intention to expand this to include a detailed vision of writing and authorship. Follow the process into the Conscious Writing Sanctuary and when you are settled there:

- Reflect on your core passion as well as the specific purpose you want your writing to serve – for you and for your readers.

- Consider: what is your *true* motivation? Objectives? Outcome?

- Put all of this together and craft a vision of writing and authorship that is authentic to you at the deepest levels.

- Create a mind map or write your reflections down in your Conscious Writing Journal.

- Review what you've written as your journey unfolds and revise your responses as, when and if you feel the need to do so.

## 2. Who?

The second question to address during the preparation stage is *who* we're writing for. As Conscious Writers, we work from the inside out and always begin by following the promptings of our heart and soul. If we're aiming for publication, we also need to add our audience into the mix at an early stage.

Our chances of publishing success are greatly enhanced when the stories we're passionate about sharing resonate closely with the interests of readers. Reflecting on our readership enables us to take our readers' requirements into account as we craft the way our words express our ideas.

# Dive in

Go through the Conscious Writing process and set the intention to answer the following questions:

- Who do I want to serve with my ideas, insights and stories?

- Who do I want to spend time with over the long term?

- What experience do I want these people to have from reading my blog or book?

Map or write your answers, and revise or sharpen your focus at a later date if necessary.

## Stage 2: Inspiration

Traditional views of the writing process usually start here and focus on a mix of brainstorming and planning. In Conscious Writing we call this stage 'Inspiration' to remind ourselves that we're involved in so much more than an intellectual exercise.

This stage includes deciding on our topic, developing it and determining our approach to implementing it on the page. We may also use reading and research to supplement and support our own ideas.

The 'Dive in' practices from Parts I and II lead us to have an abundance of ideas *and* the ability to sift through them to discover what truly makes our heart sing. This is how we answer the next most important question: *What are we going to write about*

At this point, our response ideally needs to be relatively specific in terms of what approach to our chosen topic will be original to us. Choosing a *conscious* approach to the creative writing process is an example in relation to this book.

The time we spend in the inspiration stage ranges from minutes to weeks, months and years, depending on whether we're working on a blog post or a major book project. The depth and quality of our immersion in inspiration is more important than the duration, and this is where the Conscious Writing process supports us with direct access to the levels of clarity we need.

# Dive in

- If you're still working on the question of what to write, take yourself back to the Conscious Writing Sanctuary now and ask for insight to shed light on what subject and approach ignites your creative fire.

- Use free writing to work your way towards a point where a decision *feels* right and creates a flutter of excitement in you.

- If you've been going round and round this question for a long time, give yourself permission to make a decision that is *good enough for now*. Sometimes you just need to dive in and commit to something in order to move forwards, even if it requires fine-tuning later. You may discover it's a stepping stone to your real focus, which you might never have found had you not been prepared to trust the process.

- Finally, on a fresh page, write a paragraph or two that summarizes what you've decided to write and the core message you intend to convey.

Inspiration is required to develop ideas throughout the writing process, so we need to establish and maintain effective habits right from the start. In addition to the practices we've already covered, the Conscious Writing approach to this stage of pre-writing also includes:

### 1. Capturing ideas as soon as they arrive and storing the snippets in a safe place.

It's no good thinking you'll write an idea down later, even if it arrives at an inconvenient time. It's likely to evaporate in the mists of whatever content the next moment includes.

Place a pen and paper by your favourite chair, carry a notebook wherever you go or use a voice recorder to ensure that whatever arises in your conscious awareness is saved.

Keep all of your notes in a safe place, such as a coloured folder for each topic for which you're receiving ideas.

### 2. Lay out the pieces for a multi-sensory review.

When you're ready to take the next step, use a multi-sensory approach to combine the fragments you've captured into a possible whole.

See this as a work in progress rather than a final version, as it will undoubtedly develop along the way. Douglas Adams acknowledged the unfolding process by stating, 'I may not have gone where I intended to go, but I think I have ended up where I needed to be.'

Trust the process and give yourself an accurate starting-point by spreading the notes out in front of you for a multi-sensory review. Scan the ideas you've captured to see if you've repeated one of them using different words or have lots of ideas showing up on a specific aspect of your topic, which might indicate an area of emphasis.

Look for underlying patterns and move the pieces around physically to combine related ideas. Stretch your intuitive capacity to *feel* for the harmony these individual notes will potentially make. Use the Conscious Writing practices and process to develop your ability to *feel* the energy beyond the words and ideas.

### 3. Create a living blueprint by consciously mapping and/or outlining the flow.

Working with the subtle realms of feeling, energy and intuition alongside tangible actions in the physical world are an integral part of Conscious Writing.

Here I invite you to play with a possibility. Act as if you can consciously create an energetic blueprint of the blog or section of your book you're working on *while you collate your ideas into a mind map or plan the flow of your outline.* Work with the details simultaneously at both levels – in your mind's eye and on the page – and allow them to flow freely, one into the other.

To some degree, this happens naturally given the energetic nature of thought, as we've already explored. Adding awareness to the process simply sharpens your focus and provides you with a subtle living blueprint that becomes a touchstone of integrity for the accuracy of the words you write in the next stage and beyond.

## Stage 3: First Draft

Following this process leads directly into first-draft writing, where we meet the proverbial blank page. Yet the first two stages allow us to begin the process of developing a relationship with our content that we continue to build on through to completion. As a result, in the subtle realms the essence of our ideas already exists. Russian author Vladimir Nabokov went so far as to proclaim that, 'The pages are still blank, but there is a miraculous feeling of the words being there, written in invisible ink and clamouring to become visible.' Our task now is to transform our ideas into words that are visible on the page.

With our living blueprint to guide us, first-draft Conscious Writing is like downloading content with the emphasis on writing freely without censorship. We balance the focus and intentions we've set with the flow of pouring words onto the page, and dive into writing that develops the detail and shapes our ideas as they unfold. Sometimes we stray from the central theme and discover a new angle that weaves beautifully back in; at other times we find that taking a byway leads to a dead end, so we need to retrace our steps to get back on track. Either way, at this stage we need to remain open to all possibilities.

Perfection has no place here, because it's all still work in progress. As we embrace the chaos that's a natural part of the process, we learn to trust that it *will* come together if we stay on track and keep showing up. In fact it's creatively liberating to let go of the need for precision when it comes to grammar, punctuation and spelling as we prioritize the integrity and flow of the content. Ray Bradbury points us to first-draft freedom with the advice to 'Let the world burn through you. Throw the prism light, white hot, on paper.'

Some writers prefer not to plan anything at all and instead simply 'free write' their way to the end of a rough first draft. This method of 'throwing snow at the wall to see what sticks' certainly works, especially when the writing itself is used as a way of exploring ideas from the ground up. As long as we allow time for the extensive work that will be required to sort through the raw material and extract the gold, this approach is a valid option for first-draft writing.

A rough first draft includes all of our main ideas and the components we want our book to have – imagery, metaphors, stories, examples, instructions and more. However, the details aren't yet refined or in their final form. The main advice given to writers at this stage is not to edit at the same time as drafting, which works well for most writers most of the time. However, as Conscious Writers we are always free to break the rules if it suits our purpose and works for us!

If we've purposefully created an energetic blueprint to guide us, we may find that some degree of refinement along the way *is* required. If we discover a troubling level of discord in certain first draft sections, for example, it may affect how we develop our writing from this point on. In which case, giving ourselves permission to take appropriate action to fine-tune the rough draft at least to some degree allows there to be a cumulative build-up of resonance as our writing unfolds and the book takes shape. The only proviso is that we need to avoid the trap of striving for perfection. If we find ourselves spending excessive time on one particular section, we simply need to move on and return to review it with fresh eyes at a later stage.

# Dive in

- Follow the Conscious Writing process into the sanctuary and write your first draft freely. Repeat regularly until completion.

## Stage 4: Refine and Revise

'All the words I use in my stories can be found in the dictionary – it's just a matter of arranging them into the right sentences.' Somerset Maugham sums up the refining and revising stage with this simple statement in which a multitude of complex layers are camouflaged. Whether we've written our first draft straight through to completion or refined some of our writing along the way, at this point we undertake a full review of every aspect of our work so far.

A fresh perspective is an absolute requirement for refining and revising, so we need to take a break and return to the page with clarity of vision as well as our intuitive and feeling senses sharpened. The practices from Parts I and II, along with the Conscious Writing process itself, provide us with a choice of options to achieve the lucidity we need at this point.

Printing out what we've written also makes a significant contribution to this stage of the process, as it immediately provides an opportunity for us to focus on the eloquence and accuracy of our expression in a different way. With a red pen at the ready, our creative reworking can begin.

The following core questions form the basis of the refinement and revision our first draft undoubtedly requires:

### 1. Content

- Are we on track with our original intention and the core message we set out to share through our ideas and stories?

- Will the sequence make sense to our readers and have we maintained relevance and integrity throughout?

- Have we been consistent and avoided repeating or contradicting ourselves?

- Do we need to delete sentences or sections that are simply not required or add more in to support our case?

- Have we achieved a clear and congruent flow from start to finish?

## 2. Language

- Do our words accurately reflect the living reality towards which they point?

- Have we used a rich and diverse selection of words that lead our readers to layers beyond the surface meaning of each one?

- Are the connections clear and varied to support the flow of the reading experience?

- Does the rhythm of language match the pace of the content with short and long sentences for variety and emphasis?

- Have we stretched our creative ability to express our essential impulse vividly so it truly reaches the hearts and minds of our readers?

For writers who wish to delve more deeply into this topic, Stephen Harrod Buhner provides an impressive array of detail in his book *Ensouling Language* and eloquently addresses each level of potential review.[1]

Breaking the whole into the component parts can be immensely useful, especially when we're learning our craft. Yet the more we develop our abilities as Conscious Writers, the more we're likely to *feel* the subtle nuances of the relationship between content and language, rhythm and flow, and intuitively sense when our writing is on, or off, the beat. The most effective combination for polishing our work comes from a mix of understanding the writing craft and developing awareness of the energetic integrity required to reflect our original purpose.

Ultimately, reworking our text is like composing a symphony using the instruments and melodies we introduced in the first draft. Each component of our writing can be seen as a section of the orchestra, which we raise to a crescendo and fade out to silence in a multi-layered musical extravaganza. Eventually we discover the harmonies we need for our words to ring true in our readers' ears.

# Dive in

- Print out the first draft of the writing you want to review.

- Visit the Conscious Writing Sanctuary and set the intention to see and feel what needs to be done to craft your work into a refined form.

- Use the questions on content and language for guidance and mark your amendments directly onto your printed pages for typing up later.

- Repeat as required.

## Stage 5: Edit and Complete

We now reach the final phases of the writing process. Here we focus on the line-by-line detail of our reworked text to correct any remaining errors and inconsistencies as we head towards completion.

Editing is essentially about effective communication and is the last stage of improvement made to our writing before publication. There are usually two stages of editing. The first is our own precise review to address how we've expressed ourselves through our choice of language to ensure that readers receive the full impact of our words at every level. We also need to focus on the accuracy of spelling, grammar and punctuation as part of this concluding assessment of clarity and style.

If we're writing a book or other materials for publication, the second edit will be done by a professional once we've polished our work to the extent of our capabilities. Whether we're self-publishing or working with a traditional publisher, professional editing is indispensable and ranges from major reworking to minor fine-tuning, depending on how far we've developed the work ourselves.

Good editors shouldn't change the sense of what we've written; instead their role is to facilitate the process of telling our stories and sharing our message skilfully with our readers. Editors don't always get it right, but they do bring a fresh, experienced eye to the text and inevitably pick up details that we miss. Naturally, the more complete our writing is before it goes to a professional, the less they will have to do, and the more it will reflect our original intentions through our individual interpretation of content and language.

## Dive in

- Use the Conscious Writing practices and process to sharpen the senses you bring to editing and completing your writing.

- Print out your refined text and go through it line by line, checking for accuracy and correcting as required.

- Finally, review the paragraphs you wrote about your core message and intentions for your writing content (*see page 148*). Now, while it's fresh in your mind, write a final version and summarize the main points into one compelling key sentence. This will serve you well as you take your work out to the world and are required by publishers or the media to specify in a nutshell what your book is about.

When we have our sights set on successful authorship, the last phase of the writing process overlaps with the other activities required of us as authors, specifically in terms of building an authentic author platform.

As we saw in the core principle of connection, reaching out directly to our readers through blogs, social media and more is an essential aspect of being an author today. Alongside the process of completing our writing, we need to make time and space for creating an audience and developing relationships with the people for whom we've chosen to write. Author Michael Hyatt explains, 'Very simply, a platform is the thing you have to stand on to get heard. It's your stage. But unlike a stage in the theatre, today's platform is built of people. Contacts. Connections. Followers.'[2]

Some writers still feel a degree of resistance to this aspect of authorship and see it as an endless stream of self-promotion. However, this is far from what is actually required of us as contemporary authors. Instead, we need to shift our mindset away from that outdated view and focus on telling our story and sharing our message in authentic and compelling ways. From here, a more natural flow pours through us to our readers via the multitude of online and offline means at our disposal today.

Ideally, by the time we reach the point of completing our manuscript we'll already be under way with establishing ourselves in the eyes of our audience. Now we need wholehearted dedication to ensure that the love and commitment we've put in to our writing will actually reach our intended readers and make the positive difference we've set our sights on making.

As Conscious Writers, our main priority is to communicate with our true voice from the level of our true self, whether we're writing a blog post, sending a tweet or delivering the keynote speech at a major conference. This kind of original expression is what sets us apart from the plethora of pastiche artists and allows our contribution to be seen, heard and most importantly *felt* by the people who resonate with our approach.

The Conscious Writing practices and process support us in giving birth to our projects in the world with passionate detachment and staying the course to see them through to the completion of their full lifecycle. At this point, if we remain true to our purpose at every stage, our conscious and creative focus may have already led us to sense the next intuitive impulse that will prompt us to follow a new golden thread – and the cycle begins again.

# PART IV

*Creating Your
Conscious Writing
Practice*

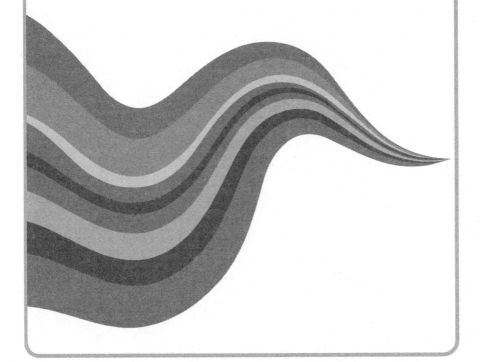

# Making a Conscious Commitment

I t's so easy to lose ourselves in the stories of our lives. We're often brought up to work hard and devote a huge amount of effort to achieving success. We stretch and strive to fulfil our ideas of how life should be, and play the roles of children, friends, partners, parents and more to the standards we've inherited, and added to along the way.

Taking a step back to review the content of our days, we might be surprised to realize just how much drama has become the norm. It may be matters of health, relationships, work, or a combination of them all that constantly pull us into the story of who said what and why we feel overwhelmed and let down yet again.

The stories play out at the level of the everyday self, where being right frequently overrules common sense and 'finishing our chores before we play' keeps us in perpetual motion. No wonder writers struggle to show up regularly to write!

## Emma's Story

*Emma had been a full-time mum after leaving her career in financial management to focus on motherhood. A few years earlier, the title for a book had come to her in a dream and she'd decided that when the children were older she would write. Now her two daughters were doing well at school and although her life was busy with multiple commitments, she felt a strong pull to do so. When a series of 'chance' events led her to a Conscious Writing workshop, her initial creative spark caught fire and she applied for monthly mentoring to follow up the live event.*

*Despite her enthusiasm, Emma found it extremely hard to follow through and carve out the space to focus on developing her ideas and doing some writing. When she finally did manage to sit down with her thoughts, she was already tired from having raced through her other commitments. She felt empty, resentful and angry at herself for not being able to organize her time more efficiently.*

*During the course of our work together, Emma learned that the solution to her frustrating situation was to create a new rhythm for her life that was grounded in a regular practice to support her in making different choices.*

*Despite an initial resistance to doing so, she discovered that getting up earlier than usual on week days made a significant difference to her whole day. In that time she did a short yoga and meditation practice before anyone else was awake. Once the children were safely at school, she devoted a minimum of 30 minutes five times a week to work on her book before tackling any other tasks.*

*Emma's morning practice soon became the most important part of her day because she was astounded at the beneficial effects that rippled out through all areas of her life. She felt grounded, calmer and more patient with her children, and she had the confidence to prioritize her writing to honour herself as well as support the other people in her world.*

*It took time to establish the new rhythm and ensure that her other tasks were scheduled from mid-morning onwards wherever possible. There were inevitably exceptions to the new rule, but with perseverance Emma realized that committing to a regular practice had essentially changed her whole experience of life. It had opened the way for her to see the tendency she had to put herself last and to find the courage to rewrite that internal script in order to write the book her dream had prompted her to write.*

# A Regular Practice

The fruits of Conscious Writing are harvested from an approach that is grounded in a regular practice, as this is what provides the optimum conditions for the seeds of creative potential that already lie within us to germinate and grow.

The verb 'to practise' means 'to repeat to improve skill and ability', and this is certainly a requirement for Conscious Writers. We know that repeating thoughts and actions creates new neural networks in our brain, and an abundance of time spent practising will hone the skills of our chosen craft and eventually lead to a level of mastery. This is why writers are advised to write as much and as often as possible; as we deepen our relationship with words, our ability to express our most sophisticated ideas in language is inevitably enhanced.

As we've already learned, the precursor to practising our craft in Conscious Writing is connecting with our soul and maintaining that connection through the roller-coaster ride of everyday life. With this purpose in mind, a regular practice means making a genuine commitment, at whatever level suits us as individuals, to expand our perspective and connect with the big-picture view of our true self.

Even if we simply spend 15 to 20 minutes in conscious stillness at the start of the day, this kind of regular practice anchors us in awareness and supports us in avoiding losing ourselves in the sea of stories that usually take us away from our writing rather than towards it.

Engaging in our own version of supporting ourselves to be present, aligned and authentic leads us to validate the time and energy we spend on all aspects of Conscious Writing. We also feel the difference it makes to our decisions and actions in all areas of life, and notice its absence when, for whatever reason, we lose the rhythm and suddenly find ourselves caught up in the drama again.

At this point, our practice shifts from being a task on our 'To Do' list and becomes something we *want* to do because of the tangible contribution it makes to our experience of life. Ultimately, the true-self perspective we cultivate through our regular practice becomes our default setting throughout the day.

Creating space for cultivating awareness, nurturing creativity and doing our writing won't come from pushing ourselves to do more in less time. Instead, it requires us to make truly conscious choices and say 'yes' to following through when the call to creative adventure stirs within us.

# CHAPTER 14

# FINDING YOUR CONSCIOUS WRITING RHYTHM

Conscious Writing draws us into a deep affinity with our authentic core where we discover the ability to stand firmly in our truth. From here we naturally have the authority to organize ourselves in a way that respects our right to write. Wherever we are on the spectrum of experience, we welcome the guidance of those who have made the journey many times yet remain grounded in the freedom to change or adapt the teaching to suit us as individuals.

Rachel Naomi Remen writes:

> 'I am always tuning my orchestra. Somewhere deep inside
> there is a sound that is mine alone, and I struggle daily to
> hear it and tune my life to it. Sometimes there are people and
> situations that help me to hear my note more clearly; other
> times, people and situations make it harder for me to hear. A
> lot depends on my commitment to listening and my intention
> to stay coherent with this note. It is only when my life is
> tuned to my note that I can play life's mysterious and holy
> music without tainting it with my own discordance, my own
> bitterness, resentment, agendas, and fears.'[1]

This expressive piece beautifully reflects the essential aspects of Conscious Writing. Listening to our authentic 'note' enables us to write from the level of our true self without our work being tainted by the 'agendas and fears' of the everyday self. It also echoes the importance of forging our own path as Conscious Writers and finding a rhythm that works for us with the awareness that not all 'people and situations' will support us in doing so.

If we want our writing to flourish, we need to line up the inner *and* the outer circumstances that are conducive to conscious and creative expression. Having discussed at length the former, it's now time to turn our gaze to the latter and address the practical reality of ensuring our work is done.

## Transitions and Rituals

The Conscious Writing process serves as a technique for transitioning into the deepest and most creative state of being as the ideal preparation before we write. Most of us have many other demands in our lives, so having an effective method for shifting out of everyday mode and into true-self creative writing mode is a genuine advantage. Moreover, we usually have a limited amount of time and space, so we need to make the most of those precious windows of opportunity. Clearly, the more directly we can make the transition, the more creative and productive we will be.

Transitioning into writing mode will take longer in the early days than when we've established our rhythm and are showing up daily to write. As Conscious Writers, having understood the significance of developing a regular practice that includes cultivating awareness *and* creative writing, we'll find the experience of following through and taking action always proves the point. With practice, dropping into deep creative readiness is virtually instantaneous. Yet even with this ability in place, when we complete a section and take a break, we may require a few days to recapture the degree of flow we had before.

Awareness of these practical realities means that we can consciously build time into our schedules to allow for transitions and honour them as an integral component of our writing life.

Complete or abridged versions of the Conscious Writing process become the ritual that signifies to our unconscious mind that it's time to write. It can be tailored to suit our individual circumstances at any particular moment in time.

Writers often create a specific series of actions or simply follow a regular routine to serve the same purpose. Jane Austen would get up before the others in her household and play the piano. After organizing the breakfast, she would start her writing, which she would later read to her family. Leo Tolstoy required absolute isolation and remarked during the writing of *War and Peace*, 'I must write each day without fail, not so much for the success of the work, as in order not to get out of my routine.' Charles Dickens required absolute silence and a specific arrangement of his study and writing tools. On his desk, which had to be in front of a window, he had goose-quill pens with blue ink and a variety of ornaments, including a paper knife and fresh flowers.[2]

Symbolic objects representing the qualities we aim to bring to the page, such as truth, clarity and authenticity, can be immensely supportive during our transition into Conscious Writing mode. A well-chosen item that has significance for us, like a crystal or special pen used every time we write, will soon become an external trigger for the internal associations we are aiming for. My choice for writing this book is an image of the characters for 'beginner's mind' by Zen monk, teacher and author Shunryu Suzuki. The calligraphy inspires me in relation to the meaning it's pointing towards as well as its aesthetic elegance.

## Dive in

- Find or create an object that will serve as an external trigger and symbolic reminder of the qualities you want to bring to the page when you write.

## Two Different Levels

One of the recommendations I find myself making regularly to my mentoring clients when they're struggling to find their writing rhythm is to create two different levels to suit the specific phases of their lives.

This idea came from working with many women who were writing alongside motherhood, and usually a raft of other business and home-related projects as well. They would reach a point of regularity with their practice and then the children would break up from school and all their good intentions would melt into the maelstrom of childcare. This resulted in feelings of frustration about not being able to continue their writing at the level of practice they'd worked so hard to reach.

The details may vary; if it's not childcare that enforces an alternative rhythm it could be a major project at work or a health-related issue with a friend that demands an increase of our time and attention. Whatever the situation, the solution to maintaining some degree of progress with our writing lies in having a secondary rhythm that respects the reality of what is. As Conscious Writers, we approach this with as much presence and awareness as we're able to muster.

Paring our practice back to the essentials often means reducing the amount of time we spend on each component and simply keeping up with the aspects that are most beneficial for us as individuals. If all we can do is take five minutes to be still and breathe, then spend 15 minutes writing two paragraphs or reading our work from the day before and planning our next steps, so be it. Regularity, even at this level, will be enough to nudge us forwards until we can pick up the pace once more.

The reverse scenario applies when we find ourselves writing to an imminent deadline and raising the bar becomes the order of the day. We realize that completing our work on time while retaining our conscious and creative approach isn't going to happen unless we expand the amount of time and energy we commit to our craft.

When we're under pressure to complete, it's important to recognize that skipping the preparation in order to crack on with the writing is a false economy. Such an approach won't deliver the depth of results we're aiming for.

Instead, we can speed up the process by decreasing our other commitments as much as possible, increasing the time we spend on our regular practice and showing up to work six days a week. Having one day off allows unconscious processing to recharge us creatively so we're ready to pick up the flow afresh the next day. This level of regularity leads to such familiarity with the Conscious Writing process that our preparation time is naturally reduced and our readiness to write becomes ever present.

## Three More Questions

Finding our rhythm comes from adopting the core components of Conscious Writing and then experimenting with the practical details that suit us personally. As part of this process, we need to answer three more questions.

### When?

As a general rule, putting our writing first works for most of us most of the time. This essentially means that we ideally start the day with some kind of awareness practice and then write before anything else, including answering text messages and e-mails unless they are genuinely urgent.

Even if we only spend 15 or 20 minutes writing, at least we've fulfilled our commitment to ourselves and our creative impulse before we tackle our other tasks. Just 15 minutes a day quickly builds the writing habit we need to establish if we're choosing to take our writing seriously.

However, this approach doesn't work for everyone. Some writers love the early evening twilight zone or come alive creatively at the end of the day and well into the night. As long as whatever we choose is sustainable and produces the results we're aiming for, it's serving its purpose and should be embraced.

## Dive in

- Explore writing at different times of the day to see what suits you best. Then develop a regular rhythm based on that.

### Where?

The external environment we choose for our writing ideally needs to reflect the internal alignment we've cultivated in preparation for our creative work.

At the very least, we need to be somewhere other than our regular workspace, even if we're sitting away from our desk in the same room.

For me this preferably means writing at home, where I'm close to nature and able to immerse myself in silence and solitude at various locations around the house and garden. As my experience has developed, however, so too has my capacity to write anywhere – on the train, in a hotel lobby or in a crowded café. I simply create an energetic space like a transparent bubble around me and within it I write freely. I'm aware of my surroundings yet fully present to my work and oblivious to anything bar emergencies.

Some writers thrive in busy environments and relish the stimulus of people coming and going and the snippets of overheard conversations – all of which can trigger creative ideas. Being away from our familiar surroundings may free us up creatively. Yet, simply going outside on a warm day can equally reward us with a completely fresh perspective.

In addition to our choice of regular writing places, giving ourselves the priceless gift of time away from the distractions of everyday life at a guided or private retreat is highly recommended. A few days of deep immersion in Conscious Writing at least once during a major writing project will result in quantum leaps of tangible progress.

## Dive in

- Explore a range of writing environments to discover where you find your deepest flow and play with having a variety of possibilities to suit different times of the year.

## How?

The third question relating to the practical reality of writing is how we physically bring the words to the page.

It's incredible now to think that not so long ago all books were written by hand. To this day there are authors who prefer writing at least the first draft of their work that way and relish the feeling of a direct link to the heart. But for the most part, even the clickety-clack of typewriter keys has largely been replaced by the softer sounds of laptop impressions as letters arrive on a blank screen and become words, sentences and eventually articles and books.

For those whose experience and ease lie in the spoken word, or when limitation of any kind prevents the physical act of writing, voice recognition software can open the door to authorship.

A mix of options may well be the answer as we handwrite our journals, record ideas on our smart phones and speak or type directly onto our computers for first-draft writing and project completion.

# Dive in

- Explore a variety of ways with words until you land on an approach that facilitates rather than frustrates your conscious and creative flow.

# Five Core Practices

Finding our Conscious Writing rhythm is a process that unfolds over time when we show up regularly and commit to following through with our creative intentions. Ultimately we learn to listen to the intuitive nudges that direct us to a combination of variables that work for us. Yet after many years of personal and professional experience of Conscious Writing in action, I've found the following core practices come up time and again as the foundation for authentic success:

## 1. Cultivating Awareness

Any and all of the practices in Part I are suitable for cultivating awareness, and a mixture of 'formal' and 'informal' practice is ideal. Formal practice is when we set aside a specific time daily to connect consciously with our true self and the mystery beyond. Informal practice involves carrying this awareness forwards into the other components of daily life as the space out of which our thoughts, words and actions arise. An aware and mindful approach will always deliver the richest and most rewarding experience of authorship.

## 2. Spending Time in Nature

Stephen Harrod Buhner believes that writers must 'travel into wilderness and bring back what they find, envelop it in words, and release it into the world'. Conscious Writers explore internal and external wilderness, and are consciously and creatively enriched by the process. The ideal circumstances include solitude and silence so we can sharpen our senses to appreciate the subtle dance of life around and within us. Whether we're bringing nature indoors with plants and fresh flowers or taking ourselves out to experience the wild landscapes of the world, regular time in nature recharges us like nothing else.

## 3. Conscious Movement

We've already established the multiple benefits of engaging the body as well as the mind and emotions in the creative process. Adding awareness enhances the positive effects derived naturally from the biological response to physical exercise. Paying attention to the act of walking and conscious movement practices like yoga or tai chi creates an energetic alignment that enables us to bring our whole self to the creative writing process. The results of that inner congruence become evident from the clarity and coherence of our words on the page.

## 4. Nurturing Creativity

When we empty our mind of mundane matters, we make space to fill our heart with creative inspiration. Conscious Writers recognize the value of nurturing creativity in a multitude of ways so the inner well never runs dry. Our creative soul may be nourished by making time to reflect, listen to music, paint a picture, read inspirational literature, connect with like-minded people, cook colourful meals and more. Whatever fuels our personal creative fire, nurturing our creative soul needs to be a genuine priority so that we schedule time, take appropriate action and resist all but the most urgent intrusions.

## 5. Yin-Style Journal Writing

As we've already seen, the flow or yin style of journal writing sets us free from a rigid structure or number of pages that have to be completed. Instead, it invites us to develop a more intuitive relationship with the practice based on what is required at a particular moment. This approach builds awareness into our experience that also benefits the other writing we do. Balancing the focus of showing up with the flow of free writing, journal writing clears the path for deep creative insights to arise unhindered when we're ready to do our project writing. Expressing our concerns and capturing our breakthroughs, it has been shown time and again to make a positive difference to the experience of authorship.

Finally, we return to the point of standing firmly in our truth and respecting our right to write. We do this by making choices and taking actions to find a Conscious Writing rhythm that works for us and evidently moves us towards our vision. Along the way we learn the truth that Morpheus explains to Neo in *The Matrix*: 'Sooner or later you're going to realize, just as I did, that there's a difference between knowing the path and walking the path.'

Writers write – so make it so!

CHAPTER 15

# FACING THE DRAGON

If it weren't for the interruption of the everyday self, we'd all create consciously and write freely. There's no resistance to creative expression at the level of our true self. This is why in Conscious Writing we place so much emphasis on opening to that space of presence and alignment before attempting to capture our ideas in words on the page. So, the more our everyday self becomes the vehicle of expression of our true self, the less power all forms of creative resistance have to hold us back.

While we're on our way to that scenario becoming our reality, we need to understand that we *all* experience resistance to doing our creative work to one degree or another. Even when we've many years of experience and a track record of success, there remains an undercurrent that can stop us in our tracks unless we remain alert.

Given that resistance is likely to show up at some stage in our creative writing process, it makes sense for us to take the time to understand and work *with* it rather than seeing it as an enemy to ignore or fight against.

So what's really going on when we find ourselves avoiding our writing or feeling empty of ideas and words? Why does the everyday self invariably seem to hold us back from what we feel we want to do creatively? Why is writing such a challenge?

## The Neurology of Creative Resistance

In *Around the Writer's Block*, Rosanne Bane draws on brain science to explain how and why writers invariably feel resistance, even if it doesn't turn into full-blown writer's block.[1] Appreciating the basics of what's happening at a neurological level strengthens our ability to move around or through whatever might be in our way.

Bane explains, 'Resistance is not about laziness, lack of willpower, or the failure of intellect and imagination. It's about neurology and psychology.'

Instead of having a brain, we actually have a brain system made up of separate yet integrated areas that collaborate to make consciousness possible. However, sometimes different parts of the brain compete with each other. When we feel that we've 'two minds' vying for supremacy in relation to whether or not we show up to write, we're actually right!

Essentially there are three main systems within the human brain:

1. *The brain stem or 'lizard brain'*, which is at the core of the entire brain system and maintains bodily functions like respiration, digestion and circulation.

2. *The limbic system or 'leopard brain'*, which envelops the brain stem and enables us to feel emotion. In fact it connects emotion with our sensory perception, so that by the time information is picked up by the cortex (*see below*), it already has an emotional component. The limbic system also initiates the fight-or-flight instinct when a threat is perceived.

3. *The cerebral cortex or 'learning brain'*, which surrounds the limbic system and allows us to use creativity and language, motivate ourselves and resolve challenging issues as well as to reflect and adapt our behaviour to suit our circumstances.

When it comes to writing, the most significant potential conflict is between the limbic system and the cerebral cortex. The cerebral cortex has all the functions we require for writing, so it needs to be in the driving seat in order for us to do our creative work. This will naturally be the case when we're in a relaxed state; the cortex then enables us to reflect creatively and think logically.

However, whenever any kind of threat is perceived, imagined or real, the limbic system takes primary control. The instinctual fight-or-flight mechanism kicks in and stress hormones are released into our system. At this point, creative reflection is dismissed as irrelevant, because we're in survival mode. Our reactions become automatic and are drawn from instinct or conditioned habitual patterns. In this situation, our capacity for creative choice and innovation is simply not available to us.

As writers, the threat is likely to be an underlying fear about our ability to write – or not, as the case may be. This could date back to a single moment in time when we lost confidence following an exam failure or a critical review of our work. Similar incidents or a prolonged period of negative conditioning from our early years may also cause us to feel anxious about being judged, ridiculed or rejected.

In fact, the more important our writing is to us, the harder it may be for us to do it because of concerns that we won't be able to get it right or do justice to our ideas through words on the page.

Interestingly, we may not be aware that what Rosanne Bane calls a 'limbic takeover' has happened if the threat lies below the threshold of our everyday consciousness. Yet if we consistently fail to move forwards with our ideas, we need to realize that our capability for creative writing may figuratively be 'offline'.

The key that unlocks the door to conscious and creative freedom is awareness. As Conscious Writers, we cultivate this through our regular practice. It allows us to notice both subtle and more obvious thoughts and feelings relating to our writing, and ultimately leads us to reduce the reactive impact of the limbic system and address any resistance we experience consciously and creatively.

However, creative resistance takes on numerous different guises, so we need to be alert to the specific shapes and forms it adopts for us as individuals. This will enable us to be mindful of its presence in our writing life and then take appropriate action to release its grip and set ourselves free to do our work.

## Recognizing Resistance

Creative resistance is essentially anything and everything that prevents us from starting, developing or completing our creative projects. It is a canny, shapeshifting creature that can appear unexpectedly at any time before, during and after our writing experience.

Resistance can be understated to the degree that we may not be consciously aware of its existence. Alternatively, it can seize us with such ferocity that we feel gripped in a vice of writing paralysis, even when other areas of our life are flowing freely.

Pause for a moment and see if you recognize one or more of the following. Do you:

- *Struggle with deciding what topic to write about?*
  Having an abundance of ideas is typical for most of us who write. Deciding on where to place our focus is an integral part of the creative writing process and may take time to crystallize, often beyond the point of starting our first draft. Yet if we find ourselves going round and round a loop of possibilities over a prolonged period of time and never feeling ready to choose one, it's likely that resistance is the cause.

- *Think about writing but put off starting?*
  Procrastination is a classic form of resistance for writers, and it's one I'm certainly familiar with myself. It's not just the effort of starting to write initially, it's also the will to start afresh day after day to see the work through to completion. When we use a selection of seemingly credible reasons for delaying the moment of truth and sitting down to write, resistance is the cause.

- *Feel overcome by doubts about your ability to write, and ask yourself who would ever want to read your work anyway?*
  Having worked with so many aspiring and published writers over the years, it has become clear to me that most of us question our capacity to express ourselves skilfully on the page. We doubt whether what we have to say will be of interest to anyone and feel that it's all been said before. A typical question we ask ourselves is, 'Who am I to write a book?' Naturally, we do need to ensure that our ideas are fresh and our sentences make sense, but if our doubts develop to the extent that they prevent us from writing at all, resistance is the cause.

- *Lead a busy life yet when you have a window of opportunity find yourself clearing out cupboards instead of doing your writing?*
  Not having enough time and space to write is another perennial issue for writers, and is a genuine challenge for many of us today. We all have commitments of one sort or another in relation to family, friends and work as well as the general admin of everyday life. Having too much time can present us with a different set of issues yet ultimately lead to the same end point. When we want to write but consistently avoid it, resistance is the cause.

- *Find it hard to finish a piece of writing and* enjoy *a sense of satisfied completion?*
  Author and teacher Erica Jong once admitted, 'I went for years not finishing anything. Because, of course, when you finish something you can be judged.' So many writers have a plethora of unfinished pieces of writing, snippets of ideas only partially developed or stories that lack an ending. Some of the early works of famous authors eventually surface long after their original fate left them languishing in a drawer. When staying the course feels like trying to hold a handful of water, resistance is the cause.

In a nutshell, when we fail to write despite wanting to, or feel anxious to the point of inertia, we're almost certainly caught in the clutches of our everyday stories with some form of resistance at work.

## Dive in

- Reflect on how creative resistance shows up for you. Give yourself permission to acknowledge it fully and write about it in your Conscious Writing Journal.

- Avoid self-judgement. Instead, cultivate compassion towards yourself in the knowledge that you're far from alone in experiencing some form of resistance.

- Allow yourself to smile as you observe what's truly going on for you in relation to your writing. For now, simply witness the details of your experience and record them in order to develop your ability to be aware when resistance is holding you back.

# The Inner Critic

The prevalence of creative resistance is matched by the universal existence of the inner critic – a harsh inner voice that criticizes, compares, judges and undermines our self-belief. The inner critic fans the flames of self-doubt and leaves us feeling disempowered and completely lacking in confidence.

The language and detail this critical part of ourself employs are selected to have maximum impact on our most vulnerable thoughts and feelings, and will always be targeted to us as individuals. However, the common themes are embroiled in inadequacy, shame and deficiency: 'I'm not good enough', 'I can't write', 'I'm not a *real* writer' and countless similar disparaging remarks expressed as if they were self-evident truths.

We *all* have a dedicated inner critic, although the intensity and frequency of its directives varies. The negative self-talk is a form of resistance, but isn't restricted to demeaning our creative efforts – it may include any and all areas of our lives. Writing, however, is a favourite target for the critic's derision and disdain.

The inner critic comes from a complex array of external influences and internal attitudes that are largely shaped by our relationships with others. It is essentially a conglomeration of judgements we've received from figures of authority during childhood and beyond combined with our interpretation of the opinions of partners, friends and colleagues as well as our social environment. It is a layer of conditioning that has become habitual from countless repetitions, so when we hear the condemning comments, we assume them to be true.

As Conscious Writers, we learn to recognize the inner critic as an aspect of our everyday self and realize that the path to liberation once again lies in awareness. As soon as we notice that this reproachful voice is the cause of our inability to pursue our intention to write, we need to stop, take a step back and turn to face the dragon's fire.

# Dive in

When the inner critic's disparaging voice affects your desire to write, set yourself free with the following steps and repeat as required:

1.  Cultivate awareness using any of the practices outlined in Parts I, II or III. Set a clear intention to harness the power of this awareness to remember that the pessimistic opinions expressed by your inner critic are a conditioned part of your everyday self and not who you truly are.

2.  Acknowledge the voice with a statement such as: 'I know you! You're the voice of my inner critic.' If it supports your process further, you can personify it and give it a name. 'Ah, there's Malicious Mary again!' Use whatever brings the recognition fully into your conscious awareness.

3.  Practise witnessing and observing your inner critic as if from a distance, and write the negative statements down to externalize the detail and gain a perspective. Pay attention to your inner dialogue generally and know that you are the author of your life script and it can be rewritten to suit your purpose at any time.

4.  Evaluate whatever critical comments you see written before you from the greatest degree of objectivity you're able to bring to the situation. Draw on your inner strength to challenge the beliefs and assumptions and look for their source. You may recognize a parent or teacher's voice, which should help you to disentangle yourself from it now that you're an adult and free to make your own choices.

5.  Write about your thoughts and feelings, and reflect on what else you may need to address in order to release the underlying fear that has allowed the critic to gain such influence over you.

6.  Set the intention to take additional action on any ideas that surface from your writing, which will move you towards taking full responsibility for yourself, including your choice to write.

7.  Work towards the point where you're able to integrate the inner critic as a fearful aspect of yourself that can be returned to the whole through being embraced with love.

Finally, if you're definite about your intention to write regardless of your inner critic, simply commit to 'feeling the fear and doing it anyway'! The 'and also' technique allows you to acknowledge any form of resistance that holds you back *and also* do your creative writing. As Vincent van Gogh proclaimed, 'If you hear a voice within you say "You cannot paint," then by all means paint, and that voice will be silenced.'

## Fuel for Your Creative Fire

The vital points to remember about the inner critic and all forms of creative resistance are that they are products of our everyday self, and awareness is the antidote to the malaise they generate within us.

The judgement and anxieties arise from what we've been taught to think and feel in relation to creativity and writing. As we've already seen, we all have limiting beliefs of one kind or another and unconsciously filter out experiences that contradict what we've been conditioned to expect. As a result, our experiences repeatedly reinforce our limitations and become self-fulfilling prophecies.

The good news is that we all have the capacity to release ourselves from the grip of inhibiting learned behaviour and reweave the threads that underpin the fabric of our lives. Each time we feel resistant to doing our creative work yet proceed anyway, the power that resistance has to stop us in our tracks diminishes. With practice, we become skilled at getting out of our own way and learn to transform all kinds of resistance into fuel for our creative fire.

The way we do this is to realize that the awareness we need in order to notice when we're procrastinating or filled with doubt is an aspect of our true self. So the act of noticing introduces true-self awareness into the situation, which can be enough to move us forwards. The more we cultivate our awareness, the more we strengthen our connection to our true self as the driving force in our creative life. Our true self is unconditionally free from limitation of any kind, so it's a bit like stoking the fire to such a degree that the light and heat dispel the shadows of everyday anxieties and fears.

Ultimately, with a sustained commitment to a regular Conscious Writing practice, we open our heart to integrate all aspects of ourselves into one complete whole and harness the critic's voice to sharpen our creative edge.

# Three Final Tips

When we become aware that we're resisting the urge to write, we need to pause and take three deep conscious breaths. Once we've crossed the initial creative threshold, this may be enough to move us directly to the page.

Until then, our next actions will be determined by our individual circumstances at the time. Alongside all we've said so far, we could meditate, go for a walk or engage in any kind of conscious movement to release our identification with our everyday self and reconnect to our true self. From here, the impulse to write what we're here to write is likely to urge us forwards.

In addition, the following final tips provide support for cutting the ties that bind creative freedom:

## 1. Rekindle Your Purpose and Passion

Remind yourself of the big picture relating to why you feel drawn to writing and what purpose it serves – for you and for your readers. Reread your notes from the practice on page 146 and update them if necessary. Shifting your perspective in this way will facilitate the process of realizing that your everyday angst can only ever keep you small and stuck. Beyond the boundaries of fear, there are far greater intentions to be fulfilled.

## 2. Use the Conscious Writing Process

The transition into creative writing mode can be a challenge, especially when you have a limited amount of energy and are feeling unsure about your writing. The Conscious Writing process is designed to address the whole range of reasons that might bar your way to the page. Use it to develop the habit of writing regularly, even if you're immersed in uncertainty and only have a small window of time available. Remember that repetition builds new neural pathways in your brain, so each time you use the process to write, you reinforce your ability to do so again.

## 3. Enlist Support

Writing is fundamentally a solitary process. This may suit you well. Nevertheless, some contact with other writers along the way will make a substantial contribution to your experience, especially in relation to overcoming resistance. All writers who actually write rather than simply talk about doing so know what it feels like and can provide you with an empathic ear. So, find a writing buddy or join a writing group or association like the International Association of Conscious & Creative Writers (IACCW – *see page 191*), either online or in your area. Even better, start or join a Conscious Writing Circle (*see page 192*) and commit to working with a Conscious Writing Mentor for a minimum of six months. You'll undoubtedly find yourself and your situation transformed by the end of that time.

The final truth we all need to embrace is that there is no perfect moment or foolproof set of circumstances for us to create what we're here to create. Theodore Roosevelt recommended, 'Do what you can, with what you have, where you are.' As Conscious Writers, we need to accept our present situation fully, with all of its challenges and opportunities, *and* take creative action in the Now!

# CHAPTER 16

# MAKING CONSCIOUS WRITING A REALITY IN YOUR LIFE

Our Conscious Writing journey began with an invitation, just like the call to adventure of the mythological hero's journey. Following the golden thread, we've explored the terrain beyond the edge of everyday perception and discovered solutions to the challenges we've encountered along the way.

On the threshold of our creative culmination, like the returning hero whose transformation is completed by overcoming one last challenge, we're presented with one final hurdle. This takes the form of a simple yet life-changing question: 'Are you ready to make Conscious Writing a reality in your life?'

The way we respond to this deceptively straightforward enquiry determines the degree to which we're positively transformed by our experience. It also establishes the quality of treasure we're empowered to share with our audience through our words and actions as authors.

Reviewing our readiness to become Conscious Writers leads us to make the most significant shift required of us on our path to authentic authorship. This is the transition from intellectual understanding to holistic application of the practices that support us in expressing our truth consciously and creatively in the world.

Vision and action are prerequisites for Conscious Writing and collectively provide the foundation on which our creative work is built. However fascinating the elucidation may be, if it doesn't lead to taking action and manifesting our creative writing dreams, we will remain armchair travellers who end up looking back over our shoulders and wondering, 'What if?'

This vital transition is the threshold over which we step to live the process and realize our true potential by becoming the hero in our own life. Naturally, we adopt levels of commitment that suit us as individuals, and these are likely to vary according to the different phases of life we're going through. Yet as we follow our impulse to write, we face this question each and every day: will we show up to do the conscious and creative work we're here to do? When we're able to respond positively more often than not, we know we're on our way.

The more we engage with the process and practices of Conscious Writing, the more we experience the cumulative benefits. Our ideas are enriched, our words are enlivened and our lives are enhanced.

Having dipped a toe in the water and played in the shallows, when we experience the stirrings of new levels of Truth and creative reward arising from our dabbling, we may decide to dive into deeper waters. As we do so, the likelihood is that we'll delight ourselves by discovering that at some level we've always known how to swim!

## From Separation to Integration

Initially we think that everything we do, including our writing, is separate from the other areas of our lives. We neatly compartmentalize work, rest and play, and build boundaries to feel safe and in control. We develop a 'home self', a 'work self' and even a 'writing self', which often function in isolation from each other.

Yet Conscious Writing is essentially about integration rather than separation, and the dramatically expanded creative potential we have from drawing on the extensive skills and experience we already have in place.

We've learned how effective it is to align all aspects of ourselves – body, emotions, mind and soul. Now it's time to dissolve any remaining distinctions and ensure that we draw on our full range of capabilities in our work as Conscious Writers.

Making Conscious Writing a reality in our lives requires us to remember that bringing our whole self to the creative writing process includes applying the aptitudes we have in other areas of our lives. Being intuitive about the needs of our loved ones, able to speak fluently from the heart on subjects we feel passionate about and able to organize our work effectively are all transferable skills. In applying them to our writing, we benefit from the underlying feelings of confidence this holistic approach provides and find ourselves experiencing a whole new level of creative mastery. Integration also paves the way for releasing the struggle to incorporate writing as an additional extra; instead, we fully embrace it as a natural part of conscious and creative living.

## Dive in

- Pause here for a moment and reflect on the range of skills, abilities and experience you already have that will support you in your writing.

- Write down a mixture of your qualities and aptitudes, such as being naturally sensitive, perceptive and a good listener alongside running your household efficiently or having expertise in project management.

- Now write about how these proficiencies can be transferred to support your writing. Remind yourself regularly of the integrated approach Conscious Writing encourages you to adopt.

## The Marriage of Real and Ideal

The reality for many people is that life is full of multiple commitments. At first sight it may seem that adding yet another project to a schedule that is already full borders on impossible. If constant meltdowns and fire-fighting have become the norm, a major review of genuine priorities is clearly required.

When the impulse to write meets a barrage of existing activity, we have to ask ourselves how important it genuinely is to follow through with our creative ideas at this point in time. Clearing space to turn our attention inwards and reflect on this fundamental decision is essential, as our next steps are determined by the strength of our feelings for or against taking action right now.

The inclination to proceed may be faint at first, but as long as it's discernible, we owe it to ourselves to find a way to honour the intuitive nudge and discover what destination lies ahead.

Alternative realities, such as having an abundance of free time and facing the challenges that vacant space may present us with, provide a different starting-point. Yet the principle of working with what is applies to all scenarios.

Once we've identified the parameters we're dealing with and have made the decision to go ahead, our task lies in gradually blending our current reality with the ideal circumstances for our conscious and creative work.

There's no single solution to making Conscious Writing a reality in our life. We all have to find our own fusion of inner and outer factors to ensure our success. The optimum blend is based on the five core practices of (i) cultivating awareness; (ii) spending time in nature; (iii) conscious movement; (iv) nurturing creativity; and (v) yin-style journal writing (*see page 169*). As we work our way towards effortlessly including these components into our lives to support the writing we're here to do, the following additional tips will facilitate our process:

## 1. Value Health and Wellbeing at Every Level

In addition to the specific benefits of inhabiting our body fully through conscious movement, learning to value our health sufficiently to overcome inertia and make changes where required makes a significant difference to our creative writing.

When we're dehydrated from not drinking enough water, congested from an excess of processed food or repeatedly deprived of good-quality sleep, the clarity we need for creative insight is elusive and writing becomes an arduous task.

A physical detox will certainly improve our wellbeing overall. Yet we can supplement this by detoxing our mind and emotions too, through limiting the amount of time we spend watching the news or losing ourselves online. One 'offline' day per week, or even a few hours away from media and technology, creates space for alternative activities to refresh our perspective or simply to emphasize being over doing.

## 2. Choose Priorities Consciously and Organize Time Carefully

Having explored the reality that many of our choices are predetermined by our habits and conditioning, we know that choosing authentic priorities requires us to shift beyond the usual identification we have with our everyday self.

Letting go of the story we tell ourselves about what we should or shouldn't be doing increasingly sets us free to incorporate and validate creative writing in our life.

From here, making this a reality involves learning to say 'no', being clear about our boundaries and agreeing to essential new commitments only for the duration of our creative projects. When we carve out time and schedule opportunities for each stage of the Conscious Writing process, we need to commit to those sessions and reserve them as sacred if we are ever to establish a writing habit.

## 3. Allocate the Components of Conscious Writing to Different Parts of the Day

Short regular writing sessions interspersed with longer immersions in our ideas and words is an ideal mix for us to make good progress with our work. With practice, we can successfully adapt the key components of Conscious Writing to fit around our other commitments.

In the morning, we can spend 10 minutes waking up our body with gentle stretches and deep breathing to encourage the energy to flow freely. This is ideally followed by a seated meditation practice or simply taking five minutes for stillness, silence and space before our project writing session after breakfast.

At lunchtime, we can nurture our creative soul with some inspirational reading or go for a brisk walk. In the evening, we can spend time reviewing our writing or researching content ready for the next day. Of course we are free to make other arrangements of the key components to fit our individual days as long as our preferences lead us to make sustained progress with our work.

### 4. Take Small, Consistent Steps, and Stay the Course to Completion

Most of us greatly underestimate the amount of time it actually takes to write a book or complete any major piece of writing. It is certainly true that writing can be done at an astonishingly rapid pace. Yet under normal circumstances, the depth and quality we are aiming for as Conscious Writers requires months and often years of development.

The way we achieve what may feel like an enormous task is to break it down into manageable portions and take small, consistent steps.

Lao Tzu's often quoted insight that 'The journey of a thousand miles begins with a single step' sums it up beautifully. Yet staying the course to completion requires us to continue taking single steps day after day until we reach the last full stop of our final mile.

### 5. Share the Journey

One of the recommendations for overcoming resistance in Chapter 15 was to enlist support from other writers who are walking their talk. The suggestion to share the journey is also included here because solidarity with our peers alongside sensitive professional guidance frequently becomes the difference that makes the difference to writers' success.

One of the aspects that participants of Conscious Writing Group Retreats adore is the opportunity to connect with like-minded others during an extended period of conscious living and deep creative writing. Such experiences are invaluable for boosting our commitment to make Conscious Writing a reality in our day-to-day lives once the gathering is over, especially when this is followed up by ongoing support. The options for sharing the journey are numerous and range from individual mentoring to collective encouragement and involvement in Conscious Writing Circles or other online and offline groups.

When it comes to making Conscious Writing a reality in our life, a combination of all the above at appropriate moments along the way is likely to be the ultimate solution for long-term success. Gradually, over time, we introduce more of what supports our conscious and creative progress and release whatever bars the way. In due course, we discover our own interpretation of how to apply the marriage of real and ideal.

## A Lifestyle Choice

At this concluding stage of our creative journey, the essence encoded at the core of my original invitation is revealed and now openly extended to encourage you to make Conscious Writing a lifestyle choice.

At first this may feel like more of a commitment than you initially expected following what seemed like a straightforward desire to discover your true voice and write from your heart. So let's review what making Conscious Writing a lifestyle choice actually means.

In addition to writing what you're here to write at the deepest possible levels and realizing your true potential as an author, Conscious Writing offers you a way to become the most complete and authentic version of yourself. In fact, it calls forth a commitment to absolute authenticity that arises naturally from a dedication to Truth. With this as your anchor, the storms of your everyday stories may temporarily knock you off course, but you'll always find your way back to your inner core.

Your regular practice will draw you into an increasingly profound and tangible connection with your true self and the mystery beyond. It's like having a permanent yet flexible link to the greater awareness that breaks through confusion and guides you home with lessons learned and stories to share.

As you let go of the illusion that you're in control and lean right in to the current of life, the unknown turns into a familiar friend and you totally trust the unfolding dream. You actively allow all that is to be your guide as you delight in the perpetual dance of Creation. Intuitive insights become the norm and synchronicity escalates to daily proportions that show you the way to feel true passion and fulfil your purpose. The alchemy dissolves the false façade and you see an authentic reflection in your external world as your life increasingly expresses your original being, and equanimity liberates challenge into Truth.

## My Story and Yours

You may well wonder what allows me to write with such conviction. As I explained in the preface and introduction, all of this comes from my own experience of reshaping the fundamental fabric of my life according to my individual connection with universal Truth.

This is not a transformation that has happened overnight. Since my life-changing accident in 1999, I've gradually explored and developed the pieces that have eventually created my current reality. This process has brought me to share Conscious Writing directly and indirectly with thousands of people, and now it has taken shape in the pages of this book.

It has been a phenomenal journey to establish and live a truly conscious and creative life as an authentic expression of my essential core. Once the tipping point was reached, however, my default setting shifted and the process took quantum leaps. I've no doubt that it will continue to unfold in inspiring new ways I've yet to imagine as I continue to guide interested others along this holistic path.

The range of possibilities that lies ahead of me and you as we end our journey is truly filled with unlimited potential. Regardless of the level you choose for your Conscious Writing right now, I strongly encourage you to follow through by making time and space for a conscious and creative approach to your writing, and to your life. Ultimately, this will become *your* default setting and benefit all areas of *your* life.

I thank you wholeheartedly for joining me on this multi-faceted adventure and urge you to keep the momentum going; a summary of ideas for how to do so follows in the 'Next Steps' section.

My final word is simply to suggest that the long-term success of our creative writing may not always be defined by what we write but *who we become* in the transformative process of Conscious Writing. It is the quintessence of who we are that empowers us to make the contribution we're here to make and receive the unquantifiable rewards of expressing ourselves consciously and creatively in the world.

May your journey enrich you beyond your wildest dreams!

# Next Steps

Throughout this book I've emphasized the importance of taking creative action in order to benefit from personal experience of the transformative potential Conscious Writing offers your writing and your life. Here are some suggestions for next steps to support your ongoing progress:

### 1. Free Resources and Membership of the International Association of Conscious & Creative Writers (IACCW)

We offer a range of free articles, audios and more at the IACCW, including free and full membership and monthly interviews with bestselling authors and international experts on an inspiring mix of conscious and creative topics. *See* www.iaccw.com.

### 2. Conscious Writing Journal

This beautifully designed blank journal includes tips and quotes to complement your writing experience and encourage you to keep the momentum going. *See* www.JuliaMcCutchen.com.

### 3. Conscious Writing – The Process Audio CD

Following a brief introduction, this audio leads you through the preparation for the Conscious Writing process, including the mudra sequence, and guides you through the visualization to the Conscious Writing Sanctuary. You pause the CD while you write and then restart it to complete the practice. Also includes access to the MP3 download. *See* www.JuliaMcCutchen.com.

### 4. Conscious Writing Group on Facebook

This group is for all readers of the book and everyone who would like to be part of a Conscious Writing community online. We have a theme each month drawn from the book's content and invite you to participate and share your views and experience. This is an opportunity for you to connect with me directly as well as to meet your fellow Conscious Writers and potentially set up an online Conscious Writing Circle of your own (*see below for more on Circles*). *See* www.ConsciousWritingGroup.net.

### 5. Conscious Writing Circles

Peer group support and positive accountability make a massive difference to your experience of Conscious Writing at every level. I've created a plan for small groups of committed Conscious Writers to follow based on the themes and topics presented in the book. It includes subjects for creative reflection, respectful discussion and creative action alongside a proposed format for the group to experience the Conscious Writing process together. Circles work both online via private Facebook groups (*meet interested others via the main Conscious Writing Group on Facebook above*) and offline where you can arrange to meet others in your geographical area via www.meetup.com. To access the guidelines and plan of themes and topics, *see* www.JuliaMcCutchen.com.

### 6. Conscious Writing Retreat

Give yourself the gift of time and space away from the regular routines of everyday life to focus on moving your writing ideas and project(s) forwards through immersion in four days of conscious living and deep creative exploration. Includes guided sessions, personal time for reflection, conscious and creative assignments and, of course, lots of writing alongside yoga (optional), qi gong, walking and more. *See* www.JuliaMcCutchen.com.

### 7. Mentoring and More

Individual mentoring goes straight to the heart of whatever you most need in order to discover your true voice – on the page and in the world. Anticipate a deep and transformative journey alongside tangible results that may well exceed your expectations. *See* www.JuliaMcCutchen.com.

Whichever options resonate with you, please dive in and take creative action to support your Conscious Writing experience. And keep in touch – new creative offerings are always in the pipeline!

 JuliaMcCutchen.com
iaccw.com

 JuliaMcCutchen
IACCW

 @JuliaMcCutchen

# Personal Reflections

As I explained in the introduction, these personal reflections have been written to provide you with an insight into my own experience of the topics I cover in each chapter. They're also an opportunity to share with you some of the greatest challenges and breakthroughs of my own conscious and creative journey. Hopefully they'll supplement the other examples and stories I've shared and support your understanding that it's all a process that unfolds and deepens over time when you're committed to discovering and expressing your true voice.

## Chapter 1: Presence

*The mist hangs lightly over the fields, drawing my gaze into the mystery of the moment. Crisp clarity above the wafting stream of vapour provides a rich background of all shades of green, silver, and the subtle gold of the landscape beyond.*

*The early morning moisture sparkles in the first rays of sun as the fresh, earthy scent from the awakening woodland breathes life into the world.*

*The feathered choir begins a call and response that gradually escalates to a chorus of multi-layered sound which fills the air with an exquisite and eternal song, and pours right through my physical form.*

*I sit in stillness; supremely alert with sharpened senses yet soft and open as the new day dawns. I feel the inner spaces lengthen and interruptions soon retreat into the source from which they came as expansion from the focused mind gives way to being here, embracing Now.*

*Alpha and omega blend back into one primordial whole. The 'I' that saw and heard and felt, distinct no more; yet still remains to re-emerge when it's required to craft and shape the mundane world.*

*The woodland birds complete their song and take their flight to pastures new, and I return to meet what comes, refreshed from basking in the view; immersed in Truth, my soul's restored, and leads the way ahead once more.*

## Chapter 2: Alignment

*The purple mat feels cool and inviting; my bare feet support my standing physique as total stillness prepares the way. The open window frames the early evening sun lighting up the golden wheat field beyond and casting elongated shadows from a few tall trees at the edge of the stony track.*

*Taking a deep breath in, I feel the exhale carrying my awareness down through the subtle pathways of my physical form and deep into the sacred earth below. Swirling round and gathering strength, the breath returns and brings the gift of grounded being, solid in this conscious space.*

*Suspended with the tallest reach yet soft enough to flex and fold, my body responds to the vibrant flow, and another exhale soon escapes. The 'haaa' release of audible sound dissolves the matters of the day; letting go of empty thoughts, the out-breath serves to clear the way.*

*Another inhale takes me up and out and through the supreme crown, where high above the layers of cloud a pristine clarity is found. Picking up the sparkling light, my breath retreats, enriched with more than the simple sustenance all aspects of myself require. I relish the internal space, and feel the cogs click into place. Finally the moment has come for conscious movement to begin.*

## Chapter 3: Authenticity

*Surrounded by books of all shapes and sizes on shelves lining the richly coloured walls of the library, I draw the pieces into place. Purple alliums stand proudly among the smiling golden sunflowers in the vase at the end of the table. A distant murmur of grass being mown outside does little to disturb these moments of silence before the discussion begins.*

*Having read and absorbed the aims and intentions of my honoured guest the day before, I have no idea what I will find myself saying when the time comes for us to begin.*

*The inner space meets outer requirements, and from the realm of unknowing the words arrive and pour straight through me as questions, comments, and deep reflections that go straight to the root of what's left unsaid.*

*I remain in awe of remarkable accuracy that doesn't come from me, yet is quintessentially genuine as an expression of my authentic voice as it shapes the universal flow with my individual traits. The timeless potential reveals itself as all obstructions burn away; this is the point to turn around and face the Truth beyond the fear.*

*The resonance of what's received flushes out lucidity, a vision of the way ahead appears before us as we speak, and in due course, a natural pause ... for now the session is complete.*

# Chapter 4: Balance

*The atmosphere in the large, sun-filled room is soft and inviting, yet crisp and clear, primed to nurture the creative souls of those who are yet to arrive. The semi-circular rows of deep red chairs stand ready to receive their charges where currently the space is filled with flashes of purple from the bookmarks and welcome packs lying in waiting.*

*The choice has been made; the dance and I have played as one. Soon the solitary space will welcome others who bring their dreams and take their place at the central core where opposites are no more.*

*My former swings from excess fire to watery depths now pour forth a rainbow-coloured stream that creates from both and delivers the dynamic end. I stand here poised at the subtle fulcrum of sharpened focus and eternal flow, enriched by the blend of fellow streams that permeates both inner and external worlds.*

*In anticipation of this moment, immersion in the deep receiving has flooded into form and structure, now all set for sharing freely. The laser intent required of me to release distractions and be here now is softened by my open heart.*

*At last the moment has arrived; embodying the equilibrium, the door opens and the adventure begins.*

# Chapter 5: Simplicity

*The smooth grey rock of the narrow ledge gives way to a sharp descent that cuts directly through to the canyon below. The highest branches of the tall trees seem distant from this elevated position, and in the distance, a solitary buzzard soars effortlessly in overlapping circles punctuating the sky with a majestic presence.*

*The panoramic view of distant horizons expands my internal space as the physical boundaries dissolve. Beyond the layers of everyday complexity, lucid vision reveals the elegant simplicity of what is – nothing more, nothing less. All that obscures the essential clarity has melted to reveal the clear-cut core.*

*The commitment to maintain this view is confirmed in every moment of every day.*

*I know the challenge that this presents; the valley is filled with creative projects and mundane tasks, commitments here and meetings there, the stuff of life that fills my days. The complications draw me in until I'm caught inside the web of never finding space and time to sing the fundamental song I carry deep within my heart.*

*Yet courage for embracing change has led me to the mountain scene where all is effortlessly clear and the elegance of essence reigns.*

*I take my leave, refreshed from seeing candid truth hidden in transparent sight; my open eyes once again focus on the dream of life.*

# Chapter 6: Intuition

*The heat of the sun radiating through the glass warms my fingers as they rest lightly on the smooth keys, poised in suspended animation, waiting patiently for the impulse to move.*

*My attention shifts as the deep rumble of a passing bee opens my awareness to the sounds of life all around. The chattering stream provides a* fluid backdrop to the conference of the birds that populates the otherwise silent soundscape with joyful song.

Listening consciously with every cell of my being, I withdraw my awareness and focus inwards. Dropping through the layers of thought, I open to a deeper level of listening that lies way beyond the need to hear recognizable sounds.

From this state of alert attention, insight arises spontaneously, and immediately presents itself as a familiar and complete sensation of endless deep and direct Knowing.

I feel the resonance reverberate at every level of my being and notice the nudge from my conscious and creative soul. It signifies that I'm on track despite the fact there is no map for this uncharted territory.

I follow the impulse and totally trust that wherever it leads will always reveal exactly where I am meant to be. In that same moment, with eyes closed shut, my fingers begin the keyboard dance to create the forms required of me; the words that only later will be read.

## Chapter 7: Connection

I'm sitting on the earth next to a tall tree, one of many in the wild Colorado forest where I am about to spend the night alone. My body feels empty from fasting, and cleansed like never before from the sweat lodge ceremony when I thought I might die from the searing heat and clouds of steam to which I eventually surrendered.

The preparation for this vision quest has opened me at every level.

The earlier encounter with the rattlesnake has triggered a primal fear, and as the sun sets, my anxiety rises. Every single unfamiliar sound becomes an approaching snake and nudges me nearer to the edge of terror.

As the darkness deepens, I finally lean my rigid body back against the trunk of the tree. Within a few short minutes, I take my first deep breath for hours, and with the exhale, a subtle yet distinct softening begins within me.

Unexpectedly I feel as if the tree is wrapping invisible arms around me, and I melt into the soothing sensation as the tree and I connect.

Soon, a wave of exquisite union radiates from my heart and pulses through, and beyond, the furthest reaches of my perception. My gaze *floats upwards and a multitude of shooting stars streak across the pitch-black sky.*

*The freedom of all that is permeates my soul, and restored to wholeness, I'm finally ready for a true vision to appear.*

## Chapter 8: Exploring Creativity as a Conscious Enquiry

*I am like the seed cracked open by the cold, dark winter whose harsh bite cuts through the closed form that contains the full potential and creates the gap through which life pours.*

*The literal crack on the crown of my head from a falling stage spotlight dismantles my everyday shell in an instant, yet my journey through the ensuing darkness seems to last an eternity.*

*The initial glimpse of grace becomes lost in uncertainty as my body, mind and emotions struggle to surface from the void. I am completely undone. All I can do is breathe.*

*The pure simplicity of this timeless anchor guides me into the deepest surrender where I learn the truth of letting go.*

*As the final remnants of the old form dissolve, the first hint of light lifts the veil of night. The new life of spring is stirring at last.*

*I learn to live, love and release the questions as I melt into essence and commit to expressing Truth consciously and creatively through the form of my being.*

*In full acceptance of not knowing how, a new life is crafted in each moment, and who I am merges with what I do as a genuine expression of my creative core.*

*Finally discovering the fractal whole of simultaneous focus and eternal flow, the warmth of the summer sun brings fullness where once a broken shell felt like the journey's end.*

## Chapter 9: Cultivating Your Relationship with Creativity

*I paint, dance, build secret dens in the wood and immerse myself in other realms that enrich the creative freedom of my childhood. I wake up and see* with closed eyes, knowing I am elsewhere yet simultaneously still here. It is effortless and joyful; a playful adventure of inner and outer.

Then I learn 'how things are'. Grown-ups have serious work to do and creative play is an optional extra reserved for hobbies and weekends. I become skilled at studying and working hard, yet retain the connection to my creative core through crimson hair and outrageous earrings worn with tailored suits.

I pour myself into my work, feel a deep sense of purpose and enjoy the fruits of external achievement. Yet by the time I reach the top of my chosen tree, I'm way beyond empty and my creative soul is starved from neglect while others have taken priority.

I'm given a chance to change or die.

The grace of transformation reveals that time and space for conscious and creative living are not 'optional extras' but fundamental requirements for me at every level.

Expressing the essence of who I am is the foundation of my creative impulse, and I choose Creation as the centre from which I and my life unfold.

Immense relief washes through me as my childhood joy gradually resurfaces, and I know that I have come home to my Self at last.

## Chapter 10: Connecting with the Whole Creative Cycle

I'm fired up and focused, yet effortlessly flowing; sharp as a laser, soft as silk. Three weeks to prepare a three-day immersion in conscious writing and creative living; the rhythm is set, now the details arrive.

The magic and mystery are constant companions, infusing each moment with insight and ideas. I am totally present to the extraordinary flow as content pours through me and I'm stretched to keep up. It's raw and intense yet magnificently balanced as I live and breathe the truth of creation, in harmony with soul and finally free.

At last I've learned to let go completely and lean in to the river's powerful flow. Surfing the waves of creative unfolding carries me into unusual streams I'd never have found without the surrender, eventually merging in a resplendent whole.

*Yet none of this would have arisen had I not honoured nature's cycle of creation and crafted a life that respects every phase.*

*I witness the mastery as the wheel goes on turning and yield to the seasons of life and death. As rebirth continues the eternal succession, I know that I am one with That, and commit to follow the natural lead no matter what and come what may.*

*Unexpected delights await my discovery as stillness inspires and imagination creates, finally returning to whence it came. And then the cycle begins again.*

## Chapter 11: Two Additional Components

*I'm oblivious to the intense heat of the afternoon sun as I kneel on the earth, eyes closed, immersed in bliss; external stillness in perfect equipoise with internal elation.*

*The two-hour timeless ceremony is finally complete. The Balinese priest signifies the start of the feast to celebrate the sacred marriage of the Divine Feminine and Divine Masculine within each and every one of us.*

*I remain immobilized by the intensity of my experience and surrender to the energy that has expanded every aspect of my being into the ecstasy of union. Shakti and Shiva merge harmoniously and dispel the illusion of separation once and for all.*

*My learning to feel and work consciously with the dynamic power that has burned me up so many times before has brought me to exalted serenity.*

*The ritual sequence of mudras and more have opened new dimensions of access to subtle realms that magnificently blend body, mind and soul.*

*Embodied Truth becomes the eternal touchstone as the next level of my conscious and creative unfolding begins.*

## Chapter 12: Visiting the Conscious Writing Sanctuary

*I feel a deep sense of congruence, as if the individual pieces of the jigsaw have finally revealed the picture that was always there but was initially obscured from view.*

*I've learned to feel the flow of life within, and inhabit this physical form through conscious movement that grounds and strengthens the roots of my being. From here the veils are lifted to expose the joy I once thought lost as my open heart becomes the perfect conduit for the voice of my soul.*

*My inner senses delight in the guided journey to the clearing in the woods where reflections elicit insights and ideas within the safety the Sanctuary provides. I see and Know as words arrive, encouraged by the process that combines the elements into the whole, and writing results until I'm done. I return refreshed and embrace the reality of this repeating over and over until completion.*

*Along the way, I discover a delightful cumulative effect and find myself entering the sacred space effortlessly and with increasing speed. Soon it takes a mere moment or two, and in the end I reside in both worlds as one and the same while the writing concludes.*

*This is what comes from drawing together holistic components that have led me to freedom and allowed me to taste the conscious and creative Source of all.*

# Chapter 13: Conscious Writing at Every Stage

*The first spark soon attracts another and another, arising like bubbles, falling like rain. It's now in my nature to notice and capture the snippets arriving without the requirement to label or analyse or interpret each one. The tropical shower runs its course and I lay out the pieces ready to see and feel and connect.*

*I line up the inner to work with the outer, and move bits around till the edge is reached and like attracts like in the subtle realms. The many become one on the coloured map that carves out the shape in the living matrix.*

*The blueprint shimmers with fluid potential, not yet fixed as the words meet the page and continue the motion of here and there, and sometimes not to remain at all but return to Source for another day.*

*The tangible touch of the printed page reveals more clearly what's on and off as the invisible template provides the measure of seamless story or discordant sound.*

*I journey again to the Sanctuary space and eventually the words find their resting place, reflecting the realm from where they came with maximum integrity for this stage of the game.*

*The process completes and another begins as on the page leads out to the world and the original voice finds diverse forms to share the gifts of lessons learned.*

# Chapter 14: Finding Your Conscious Writing Rhythm

*Absorption in my character's role creates an invisible edge that seamlessly fits my physical form. Inside, the illusion of order provides a reassuring retreat from inherent uncertainty, and stacks up procedures like neatly packed boxes in an elegant container.*

*My apprenticeship has taught me well. From this side of the publishing desk the view seems clear – this is how the process works. Do this, then that, and make it so; ensure it's done and delivered on time.*

*Quantum leaps and worlds apart, I've left the cast of the professional play. I'm naked in my edge-free space yet follow the vulnerability all the way to the page. Familiarity with private words does little to bridge the distant shore where others see and read and know what's in my heart and in my soul.*

*A fleeting grasp at times gone by reveals the limit of all the 'shoulds' and I'm cast adrift in the uncertain sea I struggled so hard to avoid before. The difference now is quickly felt, and seen and heard, and understood.*

*I respond to the promptings from within and craft my way one step at a time, breaking rules yet making progress and loving my journey of a thousand miles.*

*Finally I find my conscious beat, the creative pulse that works for me. It's that, then this, and then I Know; writers write, and I make it so.*

# Chapter 15: Facing the Dragon

*The rumble starts; subtle at first. I'm focused on the usual array of actions required to create, coach and complete my days, and meet the ubiquitous deadlines on my elected horizon. Then I'll begin.*

*The days roll by, gathering the moss of project requirements and new ideas from the inevitable pulse of my creative soul. I'll just do this, clear the way, and start soon after. It makes such sense, I'm taken in; but feel the ground shift underfoot.*

*My blinkered eyes resist the view yet still I'm drawn by unseen threads towards the beast's creative lair. The scorching heat reveals the source of hidden fears wrapped up in scales.*

*I stumble first then catch my breath; and all at once my passion rises to meet the test. At last the point is loud and clear; I recognize and feel the roar, then turn to face the dragon's fire.*

*My purpose punctures through the haze and glistening wings are soon revealed; the wisdom of the primal force is rich with treasure beyond the blaze.*

*I shed the skin that's kept me stuck in silent and habitual grooves, and emerge transformed to meet my fate.*

*As I befriend my former foe and harness it to serve my vision, respectfully we understand and feel the strong uniting force; together as we trust in Truth, we find our way and complete the mission.*

## Chapter 16: Making Conscious Writing a Reality in Your Life

*The final exhale carries me over the invisible edge and into the darkness of the gaping abyss. Suspended in the vast open space, I look fearlessly into the faceless face of death itself.*

*The distant proximity fills me with awe and time stands still as recognition reveals the ultimate Truth. The eternal moment instantly dissolves the residual froth of false perception and all that's left is the naked core that's one and the same with all that is.*

*The shimmering light around the portal beckons for me to return once more. I accept my fate; proceeding further is not for now.*

*The permanence of the internal shift from meeting the mystery like never before vibrates through every single cell and all the small stuff falls away. The ease from here for me to say a resounding and full-bodied 'Yes!' to being here and in the Now, embrace the work I need to do.*

*Slicing through the mundane mix like hot knives melting butter blocks, the way is cleared for me to take the single steps towards the end to complete my conscious and creative task.*

*The form lies here for all to feel whatever value fits the shape each individual purpose needs. From heart to heart are offerings made; and hope exists for deep insight to lead the way for creative souls to feel the force that lies within, and know the end is just the start of all that is as yet to be.*

⌣

# Endnotes

## Preface

1.  McCutchen, Julia (2004), *The Writer's Journey: From Inspiration to Publication*, Wiltshire: Firefly Media, http://www.iaccw.com/74/the-writers-journey [accessed 17 February 2015]

## Introduction

1.  Campbell, Joseph (1973), *The Hero with a Thousand Faces*, New Jersey: Bollingen Series XVII, Princeton University Press

2.  *Ensouling Language* by Stephen Harrod Buhner, published by Inner Traditions International and Bear & Company, © 2010. All rights reserved. http://www.Innertraditions.com. Reprinted with permission of publisher.

## *Part I*

### Who Are You Before the Writing Begins?

1.  Poonja, Sri H. W. L. (2000), *This: Poems and Prose of Dancing Emptiness*, Boston: Red Wheel/Weiser, LLC

2.  Tzu, Lao (2002), *Tao Te Ching*, Dale, Ralph Alan, A New Translation & Commentary, London: Watkins

3.  Sri Chinmoy, *Earth's Cry Meets Heaven's Smile*, Part 1, 1974

4.  Ardagh, Arjuna (2005), *The Translucent Revolution*, California: New World Library

### Chapter 1. Presence

1.  Tolle, Eckhart (1999), *The Power of Now*, California: New World Library

2.  Kabat-Zinn, Jon (1990), *Full Catastrophe Living*, London: Piatkus/Little, Brown Group

3.    Kabat-Zinn, Jon (2012), *Mindfulness for Beginners*, Colorado: Sounds True, Inc.

4.    Tolle, Eckhart (2003), *Stillness Speaks*, California: New World Library

## Chapter 2. Alignment

1.    Leung *et al* (2012), 'Embodied metaphors and creative "acts"', *Psychological Science*, http://pss.sagepub.com/content/23/5/502.short [accessed 17 February 2015]

2.    Anderson, Adam K. (2009), 'Seeing positive: positive mood enhances visual cortical encoding', American Psychological Association, http://www.apa.org/science/about/psa/2009/07/sci-brief.aspx [accessed 17 February 2015]

3.    Nakamura, J., and Csikszentmihalyi, M. (2001), 'Flow Theory and Research' in C. R. Snyder, Erik Wright and Shane J. Lopez, *Handbook of Positive Psychology*, Oxford: Oxford University Press, pp. 195–206

## Chapter 3. Authenticity

1.    Brown, Brené (2010) *The Gifts of Imperfection: Let Go of Who You Think You're Supposed to Be and Embrace Who You Are*, Minnesota: Hazelden Publishing

2.    Cited in Wright, Karen (2008), 'Dare to be yourself', *Psychology Today*, http://www.psychologytoday.com/articles/200804/dare-be-yourself [accessed 17 February 2015]

## Chapter 4. Balance

1.    Goleman, PhD, Daniel (2011), 'New insights on the creative brain', *Psychology Today*, http://www.psychologytoday.com/blog/the-brain-and-emotional-intelligence/201108/new-insights-the-creative-brain [accessed 17 February 2015]

2.    Kaufman, Scott Barry (2013), 'The real neuroscience of creativity', *Scientific American*, http://blogs.scientificamerican.com/beautiful-minds/2013/08/19/the-real-neuroscience-of-creativity/ [accessed 17 February 2015]

## Chapter 5. Simplicity

1.    Babauta, Leo (2005), *Zen Habits*, http://zenhabits.net/ [accessed 17 February 2015]

## Chapter 6. Intuition

1.    Wikipedia, 'Intuition', http://en.wikipedia.org/wiki/Intuition_%28psychology%29 [accessed 17 February 2015]

2.    Wikipedia, 'Perception', http://en.wikipedia.org/wiki/Perception [accessed 17 February 2015]

3.    Sundem, Garth (2014), 'Intuition, emotion-based learning & the Iowa gambling task', *Psychology Today*, http://www.psychologytoday.com/blog/brain-

trust/201402/intuition-emotion-based-learning-the-iowa-gambling-task [accessed 17 February 2015]

4.  Rider, Karen M. (2010), 'Grace, power and choice: an interview with mystical Caroline Myss', *Aspire Magazine,* http://www.aspiremag.net/grace-power-and-choice-an-interview-with-mystical-caroline-myss [accessed 17 February 2015]; *see also* http://karenmrider.com/

5.  Quoted in *Ensouling Language* by Stephen Harrod Buhner, published by Inner Traditions International and Bear & Company, © 2010. All rights reserved. http://www.Innertraditions.com. Reprinted with permission of publisher.

6.  Coelho, Paulo (1995), *The Alchemist,* London: HarperCollins

## Chapter 7. Connection

1.  Seppälä, PhD, Emma M. (2012), 'Connect to thrive', *Psychology Today,* http://www.psychologytoday.com/blog/feeling-it/201208/connect-thrive [accessed 17 February 2015]

2.  Watts, Alan (1999), *The Way of Zen,* London: Vintage Books

3.  Walters, Jennipher, 'Why getting outside is so good for you', http://www.sparkpeople.com/resource/wellness_articles.asp?id=1680 [accessed 17 February 2015]

4.  Ekman, Eve (2012), 'Does nature make you more mindful?', *Greater Good,* http://greatergood.berkeley.edu/article/research_digest/does_nature_make_you_more_mindful [accessed 17 February 2015]

## *Part II*

## Chapter 8. Exploring Creativity as a Conscious Enquiry

1.  May, Rollo (1994), *The Courage to Create,* London: W. W. Norton & Co. Ltd

2.  Wikipedia, 'Thinking Outside the Box, Nine Dots Puzzle', http://en.wikipedia.org/wiki/Thinking_outside_the_box [accessed 17 February 2015]

3.  Rilke, Rainer Maria (1993), *Letters to a Young Poet,* London: W. W. Norton & Co. Ltd

4.  Ulrich, David (2002), *The Widening Stream,* Oregon: Beyond Words Publishing.

5.  This quotation is often attributed to Goethe but according to the Goethe society, that is not correct. Their explanation is at http://www.goethesociety.org/pages/quotescom.html [Accessed 17 February 2015].

6.  Goswami, PhD, Amit (2014), *Quantum Creativity,* London: Hay House

## Chapter 9. Cultivating Your Relationship with Creativity

1.  Robinson, Ken (2006), 'How Schools Kill Creativity', TED, http://www.ted.com/talks/ken_robinson_says_schools_kill_creativity [accessed 17 February 2015]

2.  Lickerman, MD, Alex (2011), 'The two kinds of belief', *Psychology Today*, http://www.psychologytoday.com/blog/happiness-in-world/201104/the-two-kinds-belief [accessed 17 February 2015]

3.  Lubbock, Philippa (2010), *Life Alignment: Heal Your Life & Discover Your Soul's True Purpose*, London: Watkins Publishing. *See also* www.life-alignment.com [accessed 17 February 2015].

4.  Brinol *et al*, Pablo (2013), *Treating Thoughts as Material Objects Can Increase or Decrease their Impact on Evaluation*, Ohio State University: Psychological Science, http://pss.sagepub.com/content/early/2012/11/21/0956797612449176 [accessed 17 February 2015]

5.  Wikipedia, 'Neuroplasticity', http://en.wikipedia.org/wiki/Neuroplasticity [accessed 17 February 2015]

## Chapter 10. Connecting with the Whole Creative Cycle

1.  *The Free Dictionary*, 'Inspiration', http://www.thefreedictionary.com/inspiration [accessed 17 February 2015]

2.  Wallas, G. (1926), *The Art of Thought*, New York: Harcourt, Brace & Company; reissued 2014, Tunbridge Wells: Solis Press

## *Part III*

## Chapter 11. Two Additional Components

1.  Linda Madani (2012), *Intuitive Flow,* http://www.intuitiveflow.com/ [accessed 17 February 2015]

2.  *Encyclopedia Brittanica* (2014), 'Mudra', http://www.britannica.com/EBchecked/topic/396017/mudra [accessed 17 February 2015]

3.  HealthandYoga.com, 'Mudras', http://www.healthandyoga.com/html/meditation/mudras.aspx [accessed 17 February 2015]

4.  Kundaliniyoga.org, 'Mudras', http://www.kundaliniyoga.org/mudras.html [accessed 17 February 2015].

5.  Joythroughyoga.com, 'Mudras', http://www.joythruyoga.com/mudras.html [accessed 17 February 2015]

6.  National Institute of Health (2009), 'Words and gestures are translated by same brain regions', http://www.nih.gov/researchmatters/november2009/11162009gesture.htm [accessed 17 February 2015]

7.  NLP World, 'Anchoring', http://www.nlpworld.co.uk/nlp-glossary/a/anchoring/ [accessed 17 February 2015]

8.  Coren, PhD, FRSC, Stanley (2010), 'Reward training vs discipline-based dog training, *Psychology Today*, http://www.psychologytoday.com/blog/canine-corner/201012/reward-training-vs-discipline-based-dog-training [accessed 17 February 2015]

9.  Hussey, Ivan, *Moods, Broods and Interludes,* http://www.celloman.co.uk/celloman_recordings/moods-broods-interludes/ [accessed 17 February 2015]

10. Niles, PhD, Frank (2011), 'How to use visualization to achieve your goals', *Huffington Post Healthy Living*, http://www.huffingtonpost.com/frank-niles-phd/visualization-goals_b_878424.html [accessed 17 February 2015]

11. Begley, Sharon (2007), 'The brain: how the brain rewires itself', *Time* magazine, http://content.time.com/time/magazine/article/0,9171,1580438,00.html [accessed 17 February 2015]

12. Wikipedia, 'Creative Visualization', http://en.wikipedia.org/wiki/Creative_visualization [accessed 17 February 2015]

## Chapter 12. Visiting the Conscious Writing Sanctuary

1.  Semko, Tao, 'Yogi, teacher, author, publisher', www.taosemko.com [accessed 17 February 2015]

## Chapter 13. Conscious Writing at Every Stage

1.  *Ensouling Language* by Stephen Harrod Buhner, published by Inner Traditions International and Bear & Company, © 2010. All rights reserved. http://www.Innertraditions.com. Reprinted with permission of publisher.

2.  Hyatt, Michael (2012), *Platform: Get Noticed in a Noisy World*, Tennessee: Thomas Nelson

## *Part IV*

## Chapter 14. Finding Your Conscious Writing Rhythm

1.  Remen, Rachel Naomi (2001), *My Grandfather's Blessings: Stories of Strength, Refuge, and Belonging*, New York City: Riverhead, p. 49

2.  Curry, Mason (2013), *Daily Rituals: How Great Minds Make Time, Find Inspiration, and Get to Work*, London: Picador, UK

## Chapter 15. Facing the Dragon

1.  Bane, Rosanne (2012), *Around the Writer's Block*, New York City: Tarcher/Penguin

# ACKNOWLEDGEMENTS

In most books, the acknowledgements are a sea of unknown names connected by genuine heartfelt gratitude that shines brightly from the author's recognition of the contribution each person has made to their book.

For me, this takes the form first and foremost of inexpressible yet open-hearted honouring of greater awareness as the source of my inner access to conscious and creative inspiration, insights and ideas. I'm somewhat in awe of the intensely challenging and richly rewarding process of having written this book from the deepest inside-out space it has been possible for me to inhabit at this time.

The reflection of the whole in the outer world has shown me that I'm on track with writing what I'm here to write right now, and I'm sincerely grateful for the significant contribution that has made to my experience, and hopefully to the end result also.

It may seem strange to acknowledge with full appreciation the conscious and creative portfolio life I now lead that has enabled me to prioritize conscious living and creative expression in all areas of my life, including writing. Yet the reality of years gone by simply wouldn't have allowed such 'luxuries'!

When it comes to thanking the multitude of creative souls I've had the good fortune to meet and work with over the years, I'm indebted to those who have trusted me to guide them through realms far beyond the written word. Individual mentoring clients, members of the International Association of Conscious & Creative Writers (IACCW), participants at live events and Conscious Writing retreats have all contributed more than they'll ever know by reflecting back to me that this approach truly works. The confidence to express my truth via the written word has been boosted immeasurably from witnessing exceptional outcomes.

As for the means by which this book has found its way into your hands, I'm genuinely delighted to have had the opportunity to work with the exceptionally talented team at Hay House. Heartfelt thanks to Michelle Pilley and everyone involved for understanding my intentions, believing in the value of this work and seeing it through to completion so expertly. Thank you also to Louise Hay and Reid Tracy for your vision and action to create such a vibrant, cutting-edge independent publishing house, which is totally on the pulse as a respected international curator of content.

My final expression of gratitude is to you for reading this far and remaining open to the possibilities I've shared within these pages. Without you and your consideration of my conscious and creative vision, the words remain as nothing more than black shapes on the page. The greatest acknowledgement of all will come when you apply the teaching and benefit from the inevitable impact it will have on your writing and in your life. The conscious and creative ripples that will be sent out to the world in the process are worth every second required to make it so. *Namaste.*

# INDEX

# ABOUT THE AUTHOR

**Julia McCutchen** is an author, intuitive mentor and the founder and creative director of the International Association of Conscious & Creative Writers (IACCW).

Following a successful career as a publisher of spiritual, personal development and lifestyle books (Element and Random House), she experienced a life-changing accident in 1999 that triggered a series of major quantum leaps in her own spiritual awakening. She subsequently left the world of publishing to prioritize exploring the deepest mystery of conscious and creative truth.

Today Julia teaches a holistic approach to all kinds of writing that combines the inner journey of self-realization (conscious) with the practical steps required for authentic self-expression (creativity). She is dedicated to opening the way for people to realize their true nature, and her speciality is to bring deep intuitive insight to guide people to discover their true voice and to express themselves consciously and creatively in the world.

Julia loves working with people at all stages of the creative process, from the early days before any writing has been done right through to guiding experienced writers to shift their work onto new levels of originality and impact. As well as this book, she is the author of *The Writer's Journey: From Inspiration to Publication*. She lives with her husband in Wiltshire near to the beautiful Georgian city of Bath in south-west England.

 JuliaMcCutchen
IACCW

 @JuliaMcCutchen

**www.JuliaMcCutchen.com**
**www.iaccw.com**

*Notes*

*Notes*

*Notes*

# Notes

*Notes*

*Notes*

# Notes

*Notes*